C000224774

Greta Garbo Came To Donegal

Frank McGuinness was born in Buncrana, Co. Donegal, and now lives in Dublin and lectures in English at University College Dublin. His plays include: *The Factory Girls* (Abbey Theatre, Dublin, 1982), *Baglady* (Abbey, 1985), *Observe the Sons of Ulster Marching Towards the Somme* (Abbey, 1985; Hampstead Theatre, London, 1986), *Innocence* (Gate Theatre, Dublin, 1986), *Carthaginians* (Abbey, 1988; Hampstead, 1989), *Mary and Lizzie* (RSC, 1989), *The Bread Man* (Gate, 1991), *Someone Who'll Watch Over Me* (Hampstead, West End and Broadway, 1992), *The Bird Sanctuary* (Abbey, 1994), *Mutabilitie* (NT, 1997), *Dolly West's Kitchen* (Abbey, 1999; Old Vic, 2000), *Gates of Gold* (Gate, 2002), *Speaking Like Magpies* (Swan, Stratford, 2005) and *There Came a Gypsy Riding* (Almeida, London, 2007). His widely performed versions include *Rosmersholm* (1987), *Yerma* (1987), *Peer Gynt* (1988), *Three Sisters* (1990), *The Threepenny Opera* (1991), *Hedda Gabler* (1994), *Uncle Vanya* (1995), *A Doll's House* (1997), *The Caucasian Chalk Circle* (1997), *Electra* (1998), *The Storm* (1998), *Miss Julie* (2000), *Hecuba* (2004), *Phaedra* (2006), *The Lady from the Sea* (2008), *Oedipus* (2008) and *Helen* (2009).

also by Frank McGuinness

GATES OF GOLD
DOLLY WEST'S KITCHEN
MARY AND LIZZIE
SOMEONE WHO'LL WATCH OVER ME
MUTABILITIE
OBSERVE THE SONS OF ULSTER MARCHING TOWARDS THE SOMME
SPEAKING LIKE MAGPIES
THERE CAME A GYPSY RIDING

FRANK McGUINNESS PLAYS ONE
(*The Factory Girls,*
Observe the Sons of Ulster Marching Towards the Somme,
Innocence, Carthaginians, Baglady)

FRANK McGUINNESS PLAYS TWO
(*Mary and Lizzie, Someone Who'll Watch Over Me,*
Dolly West's Kitchen, The Bird Sanctuary)

Translations
A DOLL'S HOUSE (Ibsen)
PEER GYNT (Ibsen)
ELECTRA (Sophocles)
OEDIPUS (Sophocles)
THE STORM (Ostrovsky)
HECUBA (Euripides)
MISS JULIE (Strindberg)
PHAEDRA (Racine)
THE LADY FROM THE SEA (Ibsen)
HELEN (Euripides)

Screenplays
Brian Friel's DANCING AT LUGHNASA

THE DAZZLING DARK: NEW IRISH PLAYS
(edited by Frank McGuinness)

FRANK McGUINNESS

Greta Garbo Came To Donegal

faber and faber

First published in 2010
by Faber and Faber Limited
74–77 Great Russell Street
London WC1B 3DA

Typeset by Country Setting, Kingsdown, Kent CT14 8ES
Printed in England by CPI Bookmarque, Croydon, Surrey

All rights reserved
© Frank McGuinness, 2010

The right of Frank McGuinness to be identified as author
of this work has been asserted in accordance with Section 77
of the Copyright, Designs and Patents Act 1988

All rights whatsoever in this work are strictly reserved.
Applications for permission for any use whatsoever including
performance rights must be made in advance, prior to any such
proposed use, to Casarotto Ramsay and Associates Ltd, 4th Floor,
Waverley House, 7–12 Noel Street, London W1F 8GQ.
No performance may be given unless a licence has first
been obtained

*This book is sold subject to the condition that it shall not,
by way of trade or otherwise, be lent, resold, hired out
or otherwise circulated without the publisher's prior consent
in any form of binding or cover other than that in which
it is published and without a similar condition including
this condition being imposed on the subsequent purchaser*

A CIP record for this book
is available from the British Library

978–0–571–26000–3

2 4 6 8 10 9 7 5 3 1

Greta Garbo Came To Donegal was first performed at the Tricycle Theatre, London, on 7 January 2010. The cast, in alphabetical order, was as follows:

Sylvia Hennessy Angeline Ball
Colette Hennessy Lisa Diveney
Paulie Hennessy Michelle Fairley
Matthew Dover Danny Gerroll
James Hennessy Owen Mcdonnell
Harry Caulfield Tom Mckay
Greta Garbo Caroline Lagerfelt

Director Nicolas Kent
Designer Robert Jones
Lighting Designer Matt Eagland
Sound Designer Tom Lishman
Costume Designer Sydney Florence
Casting Suzanne Crowley and Gilly Poole

Characters

Matthew Dover

Paulie Hennessy

James Hennessy

Sylvia Hennessy

Colette Hennessy

Harry Caulfield

Greta Garbo

The year is 1967.

Matthew Dover bought the house from the Hennessy family in 1959. He was knighted a few years later. Matthew and Harry Caulfield have been living as lovers for two years.

The Hennessy family owned the farmhouse before James was born in 1926. His wife, Sylvia, was born in 1927. Paulie, his sister, is a few years younger. Colette is eighteen years old.

Matthew Dover was born in 1910.

Harry Caulfield is in his early thirties.

Greta Garbo is ageless.

GRETA GARBO CAME TO DONEGAL

For Shirley Herz

Act One

SCENE ONE

In the darkness a peacock screeches loudly, then there is light.
The kitchen.
The wall is painted an extraordinarily deep blue.
A long table, some chairs, a wireless on the table.
On the table is a white bowl and in it a bread mixture that Paulie will knead through the scene.
The library is in near darkness, an empty bottle of wine and empty glass on the desk.
Colette is listening to the wireless play 'San Francisco', by Scott McKenzie.
She dances about the kitchen, a bunch of wild flowers in her arms.
There is a flower in her hair.
Colette casts flowers languidly about the stage.
Paulie's voice is heard off.

Paulie What precisely is it you are listening to?

Colette mimics her aunt.

Colette 'Is it them pirates – that rubbish, turn that radio off.'

Paulie Is it them pirates – turn that rubbish off.

Colette 'My head is opening with that noise.'

Paulie My head is opening with that din. Turn it off.

Colette has been gathering up the flowers as Paulie enters with a shopping bag.

3

Jesus, the heat, am I glad I didn't wear a raincoat. – Is that still on?

She goes to the wireless.

Why can't you listen to music for decent people? Radio Eireann – Ireland's national station, playing wholesome tunes fit for a body to hear. If you're going to San Francisco, indeed – my fist will land you there. I'm switching it over.

Paulie changes the channel.
A traditional ballad, 'Moonlight in Mayo', is playing.

If you do have to sing, sing an Irish song. You won't hear ballads like this on Radio Jacqueline.

Colette Radio Caroline.

Paulie Something to do with the Kennedys.

Paulie conducts the radio, joining in the chorus.

'Two Irish eyes are shining,
And an Irish heart is pining
When I kissed her and caressed her
In the gloaming long ago.

'Loving Irish arms will press me
And true Irish love caress me
And sweet Irish lips will bless me
When it's moonlight in Mayo.'

Paulie looks at the radio as the song continues.

Did you ever hear such shite? Turn it off.

Colette switches off the wireless.

'Moonlight in Mayo' – nothing good ever came out of it – a godforsaken county full of liars and swindlers – may I never again set foot in it.

4

Colette I bet you've never even been to Mayo.

Paulie Excuse me, madam. If the braes of Ballina and the corners of Castlebar could talk, they would be whispering my name: Paulie – Paulie Hennessy. I have indeed witnessed moonlight in Mayo, I lost my virginity there. Why do you think I hate the hole?

Colette Aunt Paulie, please, I don't want to think of you having sex.

Paulie I didn't say I had sex – I said I lost my virginity.

Colette How can you do one without the other?

Paulie God moves in mysterious ways, and so do men in Mayo. Child, may you never wander through their dens of iniquity. I've never recovered from my ordeal. But I don't like to talk about it. Take this bag of messages to the pantry. Find a vase for these flowers. Take the bush out of your hair.

Colette It's a wild rose – not a bush.

Paulie It's ridiculous in a working girl. Too fancy. Take it out.

Colette does so.

One time long ago we could have had flowers tripping us. Times gone by – not ours any more. So don't have notions. Never have notions.

Colette goes to put the flower with the rest.
The bell rings in the kitchen.

I wonder who that is.

The bell rings again.

I wonder what he wants.

The bell rings even more fiercely.

Yes, he definitely wants something.

The bell is now in overdrive as Paulie shouts.

Come down here and tell me what you want – don't ring your bloody bell – I'm not your performing dog. To many you may be the mighty Sir Matthew Dover, great painter, but to me, you're nothing – nothing but a bit of dirt beneath my shoe, nothing but a selfish, filthy, rotten git.

The bell stops ringing.
Sylvia enters the library, carefully putting the books on the floor and on the chaise longue back on the shelves.

You see, talk nice to people, they'll do as you tell them.

Colette Will Harry find if he's okay?

Paulie Likely. He's sketching him, I think.

Colette Should I run up and see what he wants –?

Paulie Leave them alone in the studio. What they do is not our business. Silence is golden.

Colette Pity you don't remember that.

Paulie I know when to hold my tongue. So should you. Have you seen either of your parents?

Colette Mammy's looking for Daddy. She's wants him to fix the washing machine. Nothing else.

Paulie I don't approve of washing machines. They dirty clothes more than they clean them.

Colette On what do you base that scientific miracle?

Paulie On what I see with my own two eyes. And don't you talk down to me about science. You haven't finished school yet, big lady. You still need to get your Leaving Cert results. There's no guarantee you'll qualify for medicine.

6

Colette I will if I have anything to do with it. We'll see then who's tops.

Paulie Proud as your old papa, eh? Look where pride's landed him. Living in a byre –

Colette Don't call our cottage a byre.

Paulie Call it what you like, but what is he now? Driving another man's vehicle, doing odd jobs about the house we owned once upon a time. No matter what face you put on it, it's a long step down from being your own lord and master.

Colette Don't worry, if I have my way I'll raise him back to where he belongs – where we all belong – the top of the tree in this town.

Paulie Forget this town and all in it. You do what I should have done, Colette – get out of here. Shake the dust of this place from you.

Sylvia enters the kitchen, carrying the empty wine bottle and empty glass.

Sylvia Why should my daughter learn to look down her nose on her own? What are you trying to do to her?

Paulie Preach sense to her, Sylvia. Do a runner out of Buncrana.

Sylvia My child will settle in Derry. Her ma's birthplace. That's where she'll practise medicine. Make a fortune out of the National Health. Get all she can out of the Brits. Rob them for all they robbed us. Won't you, pet?

Colette I always do what you tell me, Mother.

Paulie Did you locate your dear husband?

Sylvia He's somewhere about the grounds. I'm hoarse shouting for him. He mustn't hear me. Or he doesn't

7

want to hear me. When there's work to do, he vanishes.
I hope you're proud of your daddy.

Colette He's not the worst. You're all very hard on him.

Sylvia Did I hear the great Matthew ring his bell for us?
What's he looking for? Should I put a kettle on in case
it's tea he wants?

Paulie Too much tea's drunk in this house.

Colette You'd starve us of the sup of tea?

Paulie I would – excess of liquid, bad for the kidneys.
You'll thank me when you reach seventy.

Colette You would know.

Paulie Excuse me, I am a woman of twenty-nine summers.

Sylvia And considerably more winters – most of them
very hard.

Paulie If my skin shows signs of exposure to the
Donegal Decembers, it is because I am an outdoor girl.
In my day I could run a mile in less than four minutes,
depending on the man who was chasing me. Sweet heart
of the crucified Jesus, look at this yoke in his pelt.

Harry enters, naked.

Don't think of shaking that contraption at me – it will
get you nowhere. Harry, why are you standing naked in
my kitchen?

Harry I can't find my clothes.

Paulie They're hardly hanging from my lower lip. Try
looking where you left them. What else are you looking
for?

Harry Matt wants coffee – real coffee – and he wants to
see James.

Sylvia Why is he looking for my husband?

8

Harry He needs James to drive him somewhere.

Sylvia Where?

Harry Belfast, or Dublin. One of those Irish places.

Paulie You're in Ireland, Harry – you're in Donegal – you've been here a while –

Harry I'm not completely stupid, Paulie.

Paulie Harry, son, you could not spell shite without putting a 'q' in it.

Harry I suppose not. Spelling's not my strong point. Never has been. Anyway, Matt's looking for James.

Harry exits.

Paulie Tell me this and tell me no more, what is the world coming to? A naked man wanders into a kitchen – sees three strapping lassies all gumming for him, and there's not a stir between his legs. There's queer and there's queer, and we may as well take up farming.

Colette Why is he sending Daddy to Belfast? Or maybe it's to Dublin. I cannot wait to see Dublin.

Paulie Colette, you'll be straying away from Donegal soon enough – stay put for the time being.

Colette With one breath you're telling me to get far away from the town – the next you're warning me not to leave. Which is which?

Paulie Give my head peace. Sylvia, do you not have rooms to clean? There must be ones coming. He could be fetching them by car. Meeting the plane or the boat. I wish the man would let us know if he's inviting a troop of people. He has a face on him if I don't have enough grub in. Am I not a black pity of a woman trying to humour the lot of yous? I'd be better off entering a convent. Everything laid out for you, no worries, no bills, no bother – three meals a day. All you have to do is pray.

James enters.

James It's a fair few years since I saw you praying, sister Paula.

Paulie Is that a fact, brother James?

Sylvia Did you look at that washing machine as I asked you fifty times to do?

James I did.

Sylvia Did you mend it?

James I didn't.

Sylvia May I ask why not?

James Because it's broke – it's cracked – it's kaput. You need a new one, as I've answered you fifty times. You need to get your big boss to buy it for you. Talk sweet to him. Who knows what effect you might have on him? Kick Harry the Horse out of his bed and heave the dirty Derry one into it.

Sylvia Nice talk to your wife – in front of your daughter – nice example.

James She's heard worse out of your mouth. Nothing could shock her with you as a mother.

Sylvia Just as well she has a mother – seeing her father's a useless bugger.

James Unfortunate choice of insult – buggers rule the roost in this house.

Paulie He wants you to drive to Belfast –

James What – today?

Paulie It might be to Dublin – Harry didn't know which.

James What for?

Paulie He didn't say.

James Is he going with me? Is it to pick people up? Are they staying?

Sylvia He didn't say – didn't you hear her? Are you deaf as well as stupid?

James Listen to her call anybody stupid. None of your breed ever went past primary school.

Sylvia My father never owed anybody a penny –

James And mine had three businesses –

Sylvia That you squandered bag and baggage –

James That you helped me squander –

Paulie For Christ's sake, enough. Early morning and the two of you are at each other's throats. Sylvia, get on with your work. James, go and ask where precisely it is you have to drive and who precisely, if anybody, you have to pick up. If there's guests coming, I need to get this house in some semblance of order. Be about your business, all of you, please.

James Sad times we have to bow and scrape before an English stranger –

Paulie Who now owns the house – he paid a fair price.

James Our family home –

Sylvia Who sold it to him? Who had to sell it to him? You.

Paulie Did you not hear me say, enough? I meant it – enough. I do not like repeating myself, so I will not repeat myself again.

Colette Aunt Paulie's right. We should be giving her a hand. Please, Mammy and Daddy, stop fighting.

Sylvia I'll stop. I always stop. Part of my charm, isn't that right, James?

Matthew Dover enters and notices the silence, Colette near tears.
He lets this register and then comments on it.

Matthew I perceive there is unease among this holy Irish family. Let it pass, let it pass. Let harmony be restored. No? All right, then you must continue to be an inspiration to us all. You must share the secret of how you manage to hate each other so happily. Not now – I don't have the time. Has Harry given you the word?

Paulie He mentioned James going to –

Matthew Dublin, yes. To the airport. To collect a visitor. A very important person, if you please. She's staying with us –

Paulie How many –

Matthew Days? Weeks? Months? As long as she likes.

Paulie Is she –

Matthew Alone? (*He laughs.*) How appropriate. Alone, yes. Always almost. Alone. Even travelling. We must make her very welcome. You all especially. She could be your new mistress.

Sylvia You're going to marry her?

Matthew laughs.

Matthew What do you make of that, Paulie? Is there hope for me yet?

Paulie There's hope for us all. I never bank on it – but who knows what's round the corner?

Matthew I'll borrow your Irish expression, Sylvia – God love your innocent wit, no. I'm not the marrying kind, as we English say.

Sylvia I was only asking –

Matthew And I was only answering. My very important friend is also not the marrying kind. Paulie, my precious, my sweet, my Rasputin –

Paulie I wish you wouldn't call me that.

Matthew But in this kitchen you are my strange priest, I am your empress submitting to your crazed eyes, I stand in your power –

Paulie Rasputin was a mad, dirty bugger –

Matthew And you are sane and clean as a whistle, but we digress into compliments. Now, I hold you responsible for how we all turn out. Spare no expense, pull out all the stops. It's what she deserves. I will drive to Dublin with you, James. We leave now. I see you're sober, darling – sober enough to drive. James, are you set?

James I am.

Matthew Then off we go.

Paulie Who is it's arriving?

Matthew Greta Garbo. Coming to Donegal. To see us.

He exits, leaving them dumbfounded.

Colette Will she come? Do you think she'll come? Greta Garbo?

It is evening of the same day.

Harry, dressed in a dark suit, white shirt, red tie, sits polishing cutlery.

Paulie, dressed as before, takes some pieces as he cleans them and gives them an extra flourish.

Paulie Harry, you've not spoken for twenty minutes. What's wrong with you?

Harry You're annoying me – do you not trust me to clean them properly?

Paulie I saw Greta Garbo in a film once examining her face in a soldier's sword just before she was shot by a firing squad – maybe it was Marlene Dietrich. Anyway, no matter who, I want this cutlery to be perfect. So, thank you for doing a good job, but I'm just double checking to be sure it's clean.

Harry Any road, that's why I'm not talking.

Paulie I thought only Irish people said 'any road' – you're picking up the lingo.

Harry It's just that I think it's not fair, Paulie. Asking James to go to Dublin and not me.

Paulie You can't drive, Harry – James can – that's his job.

Harry I still think they should have asked me to go. I could have been there when Matt meets her, Miss Garbo. She might need a bodyguard. No better man.

Paulie If she wanted one, she would have brought her own. Why in the hell is the woman coming here to the back of beyond? I still do not know –

Harry Didn't Matt tell you?

Paulie What were you informed?

Harry He tells me nothing. He takes me nowhere. I've never been to Dublin –

Paulie They're only going to the airport – outside the city.

Harry It's the principle. I'd still like to be asked. I'm not his dogsbody. I do a good job in his gardens – I earn my keep.

Paulie Harry, what age are you?

Harry Hitting thirty.

Paulie And well preserved as he is, your lover-boy will never see fifty again. The world looks at you and asks, what does that young man see in Sir Matthew Dover? Guess what they answer? Face it – you are what's known as a kept man.

Harry You mean, a whore? No sweat, but I'm not a cheap whore.

Paulie I'm glad you've kept your reputation, dear.

Harry And my appearance. It's why I left the boxing ring. Protect your assets. Is the suit nice?

Paulie Very classy.

Harry Had it for years – still fits. I'm wearing it for Miss Garbo. Matt would like me to look nice. Everyone's dressing up to welcome her. Are you going to do something with yourself?

Paulie What are you implying by that?

Harry Nothing.

Paulie You must mean something – speak out, <u>be a man or be a mouse.</u>

Irish/Eng = to encourage some 1 to be brave when they're frightened to do/say something

*Harry removes his jacket and starts to shadow-box
skilfully about the room.*

Harry I meant nothing.

Paulie You think I should spruce myself up to welcome
the distinguished visitor?

Harry I didn't say that.

Paulie You thought it, though. Young fella, you have
been in this house two years. Guess how long I have
resided here?

Harry For ever.

Paulie Exactly. I was born here, reared here, know every
room, nook and cranny – I allowed myself be hired by
Sir Matthew Dover to act as his housekeeper and cook,
for I intend to be carried in my coffin out of here. And in
that time how many visitors have I seen pass out of and
in through these doors? Guess –

Harry Millions.

Paulie Stop that leaping around –

Harry I have to train – keep fit – big fight –

Paulie Stop it when I'm talking to you. Your fighting
days are over – get back to cleaning that cutlery. Answer
me, how many guests have I seen?

Harry I said, millions.

Paulie Not quite. A lot less, especially the ones Matthew
Dover, knight of the realm, invites. There is something
strange about all those fancy folk he insists are coming.
Few – very few – really do. Are you a betting man,
Harry?

Harry Sometimes.

Harry goes back to cleaning the cutlery.

Paulie What odds would you give me they land home with an empty car? What excuse will Greta Garbo offer for not being quite up to travel over for a cup of tea in the homes of Donegal?

She starts to sing 'The Homes of Donegal'.

'I'm happy to be back again
To greet you big and small,
For your hearts are like your mountains
In the homes of Donegal.'

She stops singing.

Hearts like mountains – have you noticed, Harry, our mountains aren't that big in Donegal? Or does that observation pass you by as well?

Harry What happened to you, Paulie?

Paulie I beg your pardon?

Harry What turned you into such a nasty piece of work?

Paulie Compared to the charmer you share a bed with?

Harry His bark is worse than his bite.

Paulie I've never been bitten – you have the advantage over me.

Harry I think you'd like to have that instead of me.

Paulie laughs.

Paulie What puts this into your head?

He does not answer.

I believe you are serious. Are you?

Harry continues to clean the cutlery.

Why?

Harry Old men go funny.

Paulie Jesus, thanks.

Harry He was married before, you know. Once before. When he was younger.

Paulie He told me all. Confessed in his cups – drunk as a skunk one night. During the war he was up to his oxsters working for military intelligence. Top secret that, dangerous secret to the wrong ears. Same war, even big shots, their guts were rattling – strict rations. Didn't he hit on a way to double his? He tied the knot with a barmaid – access to grog and grub – drop in to see her at weekends and devour all she was hoarding to live on for the other five days. Wolfed down the lot – convinced the poor bitch she was fat. Did drawings to prove it. But you have to hand it to her. Do you know how the marriage ended?

Harry shakes his head.

He found her in bed with his best friend. The man he was really after. The divorce was as rapid as it could be. I think she cured him of women.

Harry Where is she now?

Paulie How would I know? Harry, you're safe from my machinations. Believe me, while you're useful to him, he won't kick you out from under the covers. Stop working in his gardens, start looking for a wage that pays you for your hard graft – see how long you last, sonny.

Harry You still haven't answered the question I asked you.

Paulie Mercifully, I've forgotten it. Remind me again.

Harry What happened to you, Paulie?

18

Paulie has started to gather up the cutlery Harry has been cleaning, not examining it, putting it back into its box.

Paulie Nothing happened. That's why I am what you see – absolutely nothing ever happened to me.

Harry Who do you blame for that?

Paulie The cat – the dog – the rat – the sun – the moon – the stars – you name it, I'll blame it. Makes life bearable. That and laughing at my nearest and dearest.

Harry Am I included there – your nearest and dearest?

Paulie No, Harry, you're not. Don't be too distressed. Thank your lucky stars you have nothing to do with us – nothing too intimate. This breed of ours, we destroy each other.

Harry Even little Colette?

Paulie She's not that little any more. She'll survive – she'll get away. Me and her father didn't. Well, we did, but we couldn't last away from home. She will. We have big plans for that one.

Harry My dad always said the best laid plans –

Paulie Your da never met me. I know what will happen, never fear.

Sylvia enters, wearing a good dress to show off her figure, her hair neatly combed.

Sylvia Fear what?

Paulie Fear everything. What are you dolled up for?

Sylvia What do you mean, 'dolled up'? I ran a comb through my hair – it was standing on my head like a rose bush. Jesus, you can do nothing here without people getting very pass-remarkable.

Harry I think it looks nice, Sylvia.

Sylvia Thank you, Harry, spoken like a gentleman, and I return the praise. I've always said that suit is the last word – gorgeous.

She kisses Harry on the cheek.

Paulie Don't turn his head, you. Worse than your daughter.

Sylvia Does she have her eye on Harry as well?

Paulie I won't answer that – he's big-headed enough, aren't you? Still, it's a nice dress – new?

Sylvia Quite the glamour girl, am I not? I'll run off to Hollywood with Miss Greta Garbo.

Paulie Don't bother, pet – you'll never get work. There's not much call for a toothless Shirley Temple.

Colette runs in, a ribbon in her hair, wearing good shoes, carrying a silver teapot.

Colette Is this shining enough?

Paulie nods and takes the teapot.

Sylvia What did I tell you about running like a yahoo – it's not ladylike.

Paulie What would you know about ladylike?

Sylvia I come from one of Derry's prominent Catholic families – highly respected for our part in the struggle to free Ireland –

Paulie We did our bit as well. My own father and his father were known as the best shots in Donegal. We still have some of their guns. And say what you like about James, I've never doubted he was an Irishman.

Harry I can see the car –

Paulie Is she in the car with them? Greta Garbo? He didn't ring from the airport to say he was staying in Dublin. She must be with him. She must be coming.

Harry I think I might check the flowerbed.

Paulie Hold your ground.

Sylvia Should I make double sure the sheets are all right?

Paulie What is wrong with the two of you?

Colette We're all nervous, Aunt Paulie. It's Greta Garbo. She's coming to our house.

Paulie This is not our house. It has not been so for many years. We are servants now. But that does not mean we have neither manners nor breeding. Be ready to greet Miss Garbo, each and every one of us, with no hysterical nonsense. She is, as we are, a normal human being. Do I make myself clear?

They nod.

Colette I'm still wild excited. I've never met a film star. Do you think she knows Rock Hudson?

Paulie I will not warn you again.

Sylvia She'll behave. The child's beside herself.

Colette They're outside – will I run out to give them a hand?

Paulie Let your father do his job. We can meet anyone on an equal footing. We're decent Irish men and women –

Harry I'm not – I'm carrying in her suitcase.

Harry exits as Paulie calls after him.

Paulie She has two hands like the rest of us – let her carry it in herself.

James enters, resplendent in chauffeur's uniform, showing himself to best advantage. He observes their silence.

Sylvia Well, where is she?

Colette What is she like, Daddy?

Sylvia Does she speak English?

James Haven't you heard her in films speaking English? Garbo talks.

Sylvia That's right – I forgot.

James Stupid bitch, Sylvia. Make us tea – do something useful. I'm parched. Six hours driving from Dublin – never asked if I had a mouth on me for a sandwich or a drink.

Paulie What's keeping them outside?

James He's showing her what you can see of the view by evening light. She likes the look of the lake – she can swim – swam a lot in Sweden. Donegal reminds her of home – all the water.

Colette Is the car loaded with luggage?

James One big suitcase – she believes in travelling light.

Paulie Is she stuck up?

James Quiet enough. She spoke when himself gave her a chance to get a word in. Doing a hard sell on the house. I think he might want rid of it.

Sylvia Jesus, what will become of us?

Paulie I'm sure she would have more sense than to bother –

James He hints he'll offer it to her as a bargain.

22

Sylvia What does she look like now?

James Better looking than you did twenty years ago.

Sylvia You really are a gulpin of a man.

Colette Is she not beautiful any more, Daddy?

James Depends what you mean by beauty, darling. Some men settle for what they are offered, or for what's thrown at them.

Sylvia They should consider themselves lucky to get that much.

James Lucky, that's a rare word – glad you reminded me of it, I'm always forgetting what it means. I smell nothing cooking. What have you ready?

Paulie I presume her ladyship will have her own orders when she sees fit to eat. I'll do as I'm told. Not that it will be good enough for her like, I'm sure.

Colette Daddy said she's not stuck up.

Paulie She's lived long enough in America to have notions – Yanks have notions. She must be taking a long time to see the view. It's bad manners on her part to keep the company waiting.

Still beautiful, Greta Garbo enters, wearing a flowered scarf, attended by Matthew and Harry, who carries her suitcase.

Matthew Ladies and gentlemen, I take great delight in introducing –

Sylvia There's no need for introductions – no need at all. We know – we know well who this lovely lady is. Miss Garbo, Miss Greta Garbo. You're welcome – you're more than welcome. Indeed, as the song says, you're as welcome as the flowers in May to dear old Donegal.

23

Greta I dislike flowers.

Sylvia I'm very sorry. I was quoting the song.

Greta I dislike songs. Tell me you are not lined up here to sing.

Sylvia We're not Donegal's answer to the Von Trapp family –

Greta I am glad to hear it – but your hair – it reminds me of Julie Andrews in *The Sound of Music*.

Sylvia Thank you, I'll take that as a compliment –

Greta I despise her and the whole ridiculous movie.

Sylvia I saw it five times when it was showing in Derry.

Greta Is this your child? This girl? Did you take her along with you to witness the atrocity?

Sylvia I did.

Greta Then you are not a fit mother and should be shot like a dog, a mad dog. Why are you looking at me with eyes like a cow? They make me think you are going to cry. Are you going to cry?

Sylvia Yes.

Greta Good. I like to see people weep. I am a great gloomy Swede.

Paulie bursts out laughing, as do Matthew and Greta.

Matthew Garbo laughs.

Paulie Oh Greta Garbo, I'd say you're a pantomime in Stockholm.

Greta You know my native city?

Paulie Never set eyes on it. I've just prided myself always I have a bit of Viking blood in me.

Greta Ah – you are a pagan.

Sylvia She is that.

Greta I too am Viking. We boys shall get on. Mrs – Mrs –

Paulie Miss – Miss Paulie Hennessy. This is my brother, James.

Greta Our driver from Dublin. Silent, all the way. Not a happy man.

Paulie This is his wife, Sylvia.

Greta I can see why.

Paulie My niece, their daughter, Colette.

Greta A charming girl, clever looking. Get away from your parents. I did. It was the making of me. Of course it broke my heart, as it did theirs, but hearts mend. They always do.

Paulie You've met our gardener, Harry.

Greta Matthew's young lover, he boasts about you, but he did not tell me you were so handsome. Why say nothing, dear friend, about this? I have to warn you against me, young fellow. It is my great misfortune that all my life, the only men who truly want to marry me are homosexual. So far, I have managed to resist. But who knows when I might fall? Matthew, do not look so cross – I'm only teasing, old friend. Are you angry with me already?

Matthew No, my darling, not angry. Just a little nonplussed –

Greta What is 'nonplussed'?

Colette It means surprised or confused as to how you should react.

Greta Quite the teacher. You get your brains from your father's side of the family, and your beauty you get from – from –

She looks at Sylvia.

From God.

She turns to Matthew.

Why are you nonplussed, Matthew?

Matthew I was in my old-fashioned way under the impression that the host should do the introductions, and not –

He looks at Paulie.

Good heavens, what do I call you, Paulie? In all the years you've worked for me, have we ever settled on a job description? Whatever it is, you clearly do not believe an Englishman's home is his castle.

Greta You are not in England, my dear. They kept correcting me on the plane. We are not flying to Dublin, England, but Dublin, Ireland. And a long flight it was. I am exhausted. I must sleep. I really must.

Paulie Eat some food – let me feed you, please.

Greta I was wined and dined on the plane. It is sufficient. Some hot water, some lemon only. And a pillow to rest my weary head. All I need.

James You are a woman easily pleased.

Greta He speaks – he speaks. And I have to correct him immediately. No woman is easily pleased. Have you not learned that yet?

Harry Miss Garbo, may I carry your bag upstairs?

Greta I would be happy to let you do that. First I may go outside with you. The sky here is like Sweden – full

26

of stars. You cannot see them in the great city of New York. I would like to be that Russian woman who went into space and could look down on the earth – would that not be fun? Yes, I will go out – no, no, I change my mind. That will nonplus Matthew again. Can I say that, little teacher? Is it a verb – to nonplus?

Colette I think so – I'm not sure –

Greta You must tell me when I use the wrong English. Even after all these years away from Sweden, my English can let me down. I don't like that. I want it to be perfect. It is good, perfection. Matthew, king of your castle, shall you or one of your vassals show me please to my bedroom?

Matthew I will have that pleasure.

Paulie Will you be eating, Matthew?

Matthew A little something – anything you rustle up – you decide. What am I saying? A waste of advice. You'll decide anyway. Would I be wrong in saying you're already decided?

Paulie Steak and kidney pie.

Matthew My favourite – lashings of gravy. You spoil me. You spoil us all. I'm sure you've made sufficient to feed your ravenous brood. Extend my invitation to them all. I'm sure you already have. Certainly one of the charms of living in this house among the Irish. They do not believe in waiting on ceremony. That's always been the rule here, hasn't it? It was in your father's day, and your brother's day, when they owned it. Wasn't it so, James? Glad it hasn't changed. Looking forward to feasting with you at dinner. Eat up – drink up.

James We'll have to disappoint you – we'll be making our way home. We eat tonight at our own table.

Sylvia We've nothing in –

James We'll find something. Thank you for your kind invitation, Sir Matthew, but we must decline.

Greta A great hunger has suddenly hit me. I will eat. And I insist you all join me. Miss Hennessy, we shall be seven for dinner. You will see to it, if you please. Surely in his castle, no Englishman would refuse a lady – am I right, Matthew?

Matthew Greta, you are perfectly right.

Greta turns to James.

Greta Will you humour this old Viking and drink blood from my oxen? Or do I have to chop your head off?

She clips James's ear.

James Your wish is my command.

Greta Then I am pleased. Easily pleased. Sometimes a woman can be –

She glares at Sylvia.

When she puts her mind to it. I will have a short nap. Lead the way, Sir Matthew, old friend.

Greta and Matthew exit.

Colette Isn't she mighty? She speaks loads of English. She knows what 'vassal' means.

James She's kept herself well – a fine-looking woman when you see her up close.

Paulie Harry – luggage upstairs. She's fresh as a daisy, and she's travelled from New York.

James She's some woman.

Colette She's really smart.

Harry She knows a good-looking man when she sees one.

28

He exits with the luggage.

James She put Sir Matthew in his box.

Paulie She's definitely not what I expected – much nicer. More down to earth.

Sylvia Well, I think she's a bag of shite.

Paulie The voice crying in the wilderness.

Sylvia She was very cruel. Not one of you stood up for me. James, eat here if you want. Colette, we go home. Not a word out of you. We eat in our own house. We have some pride, if your father doesn't. Come with me.

Sylvia exits, Colette looks at Paulie, Paulie signals Colette to follow Sylvia.

Paulie Go with your mother.

Colette Daddy?

Paulie You'll serve Miss Garbo breakfast tomorrow. Run on.

James You heard your aunt. Run on. I'm not following her.

Colette And neither am I. I'm here to help Aunt Paulie. Let Mammy stew on her own. I stay here. And on my own head be it.

SCENE THREE

The garden before the house.
   It is a bright summer's morning.
   There is a small table with a white cloth and tray.
   On the tray a toast rack, jams, butter dish and tea things.

The silver teapot Colette was cleaning is in pride of place.
Greta sips tea.
She has her hair in a turban and wears a robe.
She listens to the sounds of nature.
The screech of the peacock shakes the cup in her hand.

Greta There it is again. What is it? It made me spill my tea.

Paulie enters.

Paulie Are you fed and watered? Can I get you anything else? Did you enjoy your breakfast? How did you sleep?

The peacock screeches again.

Would that creature not put the heart crosswise in you?

Greta What is it?

Paulie A peacock. Nobody knows how it flew here, or how it survives the wilds of Donegal. It roams all over the place – does no harm to anybody, though it does hate Sylvia. She's terrified of it. Was the water all right? For your hair? I boiled the kettle to the heat I use for washing my own. Was it okay?

Greta Is my bathwater ready?

Paulie It's heating nicely. Have patience. Let your hair dry in the sun. It will grow dry as dust under that turban. Trust the Donegal weather.

Greta removes the turban, her hair nearly dry.

Look at that head of hair. It is like my mother's, God rest her. Wonderful strength in it.

She touches Greta's hair.

I used to love combing Ma's –

Greta disengages from Paulie's touch gently.

Greta Is summer always so warm here?

Paulie is folding Greta's turban.

Paulie Changeable – even in July and August – never that cold, never that warm for too long. It's a perfect climate in its way – give it time, you might enjoy it. As I say, have patience. It's strange –

Greta What is?

Paulie Nothing – I shouldn't say –

Greta All the more reason to say it.

Paulie Strange how quickly people settle here. I've known a fair few come for a short while, and they stay – something makes them stay. You should see more of the place.

Greta I will go for a long drive today.

Paulie Take a walk too – find your way about the town – enjoy the beaches and the sea water –

Greta You like the sea?

Paulie I couldn't live without it. Once I had to emigrate –

There is an almighty clamour from the peacock, accompanied by a scream from Sylvia as she enters.

Sylvia Did yous hear that bloody creature? Did yous see what it did to me?

Paulie We were deep in conversation – so, no, we didn't.

Sylvia Then excuse me, I'll be left lying lifeless in the middle of a field but you two are going to let that mad bastard of a bird go for my throat and not interrupt your gossiping. Honest to Jesus, the way it looks at me, you'd think it had a knife in its eyes – and the way it ran after me, I swear it was going to stick its beak up my skirt.

Greta It must have a death wish.

Sylvia Do you think so? Well, if I catch it, I will wring its neck –

Greta No need to do that. There is a kinder method –

Sylvia Which is?

Greta A Swedish hunting trick. We use it to charm wild pheasants – they fall from the skies into our hands.

Sylvia What should I do?

Greta Walk naked – stark naked – before the peacock.

Sylvia In my pelt? Are you mad? That will put a stop to this?

Greta I assure you, yes.

Sylvia How?

Greta The peacock will die laughing.

Sylvia I'm going to my work. Paulie, would you mind if I finish a wee bit early tonight? I'm going to the pictures. There's a film with one of my favourites in it – Ingrid Bergman. I love Ingrid Bergman. She got an Oscar. If not two. Good day to you both, ladies.

James enters.

James I'm glad I caught you.

Sylvia Wonders will never cease – why?

James You've got to get a picnic ready. Sir Matt's going for a drive –

Sylvia Then I'd better get a move on. Can't stand here exchanging pleasantries. Wonder where I left the rat poison – though I'm sure there's some would survive it.

Sylvia exits.

James I see she's pleasant as ever.

Paulie She'll calm down.

James I'm sent on a double mission. The water for your bath's pouring. And Sir Matthew wants to know when you'd like to go for the drive. He's dying to show you the places he's painted. Malin Head – as far north as you can go in Ireland – the mountains of Urris – Stragill beach –

Paulie Would you like to see Derry?

Greta What is Derry?

James Who'd want to see there?

Paulie It's the nearest city.

James Nothing much happens.

Greta Why then should I see it?

Paulie You might be pining for the big town. Shops. Crowds –

Greta I will not go there, no.

Paulie They'll be heartbroken. They don't see much to entertain them. You might have livened the place up.

James It would take something to get a bit of jizz out of that joint. I'll tell Sir Matt it's Malin Head you want to see in the flesh.

Paulie The roads down there are a bit rickety, but have no worries – James is the most reliable of drivers. He knows the whole country like the back of his hand. You can trust that man anywhere in a motor. I'll send Colette out to collect your tray. How's your hair drying?

Greta touches her hair.

Greta It is doing well.

33

Harry enters carrying a bunch of red roses.

Paulie Here comes a gentleman carrying flowers for a lady.

James He'd better have his apology ready – have you forgotten she doesn't like flowers?

Greta It is the thought that counts. Thank you for your kindness.

James I always think there's something soft about a man with a bunch of roses in his fist. A bit of a ponce – fit him better to be doing a day's work. I'll be off to my own business.

James exits.

Paulie Ignore that bad-mouthed boyo, Harry. Always finding fault. These smell gorgeous. Honest to God, Miss Garbo, this man could grow grass in a desert. You're great, Harry. I'll send Colette out for the tray.

Greta You have already said that. Don't repeat yourself.

Paulie I won't – right. I don't want to rush you, but I'd say Matt is champing at the bit to get on the road. Take advantage of the fine spell. Will you come in straight away for your bath?

Greta No.

Paulie Right. If the water cools –

Greta Heat more. As you advise me, I advise you. Have patience, all of you – patience.

Paulie exits.

You take charge of the grounds here?

Harry More or less – James gives me a hand sometimes.

Greta So you know about the peacock?

34

Harry Our pal? Everybody knows –

Greta Why do you not get rid of it?

Harry Kill it? No one would dare. They'd think it bad luck.

Greta Why?

Harry Because it's beautiful.

Greta does not answer as the peacock screeches.

Greta Perhaps I might belong here.

Harry Sorry?

Greta How did you take to this place?

Harry I didn't – I still haven't. I needed to get out of London.

Greta And breathe pure air?

Harry Matt's idea – come with him here. I agreed. Not where I'd want to be.

Greta Which is where?

Harry America – New York.

Greta does not answer.

I was in the fight business. Good enough at it. Made no money. Well, next to nothing. The big bucks are across the Atlantic. I'd love Matt to take a chance and go there. See how we cope. He said he's done his stint in the States, but all the big shots need muscle there –

Greta Muscle?

Harry Bodyguards. Have you not had plenty? That's how I'd start off – see where it leads. Just a matter of contacts.

Greta So important in every business in America.

Harry Especially boxing.

Greta Yes.

Harry Would you be acquainted with anybody –?

Greta No. It is not my concern. Edith Piaf – she adored fighters. Perhaps you confuse me for her. She is dead – very dead. No longer warbling for France. I cannot put in a word. Thank you for the flowers. I must not detain you from the pleasure of your work. Good morning. So the peacock is safe?

Harry For sure.

Greta Even though it is not native?

Harry They'd never touch it.

Greta Because it is beautiful.

Harry Yes.

> *Harry exits.*
> *Greta lifts the silver teapot and shakes it.*
> *She catches her reflection in the silver.*
> *She whispers to herself.*

Greta Older – I must not grow older.

> *She leaves down the teapot as Colette enters.*

Colette May I take the tray? Your bath's going to be freezing. You must be drowning in hot water in Hollywood.

Greta I don't live in Hollywood any longer – I live in New York now.

Colette Do you go back to Sweden often?

Greta No.

Colette Will you head there from here? What brings you to Ireland?

Greta I was invited by Sir Matthew.

Colette Then he's looking for something. He does nothing for nobody without leaving them obliged to him.

Greta How are you obliged?

Colette If I am, it's not for much longer. I'll be out of his way soon. I'd like to see him look down his nose when I qualify as a doctor from University College Dublin. Do you think it will be wild hard?

Greta What?

Colette Medicine.

Greta I don't know – I dislike doctors.

Colette You dislike a lot of things. You don't like flowers, or songs –

Greta Seven years it takes to become a doctor. A long time to study. How will you afford it?

Colette I'm aiming to get a scholarship. The government's brought them in, if you have brains enough. And I'm careful with money.

Greta So am I.

Colette Poor people have to be.

Greta We do.

Colette You're not poor, Miss Garbo.

Greta I had to work to help my father – my family. In a department store. Selling hats. Modelling hats. Making movies in Sweden. Silent – I was your age. I could not have dreamt of going to university – of being a big doctor.

37

I was poor, yes. Sweden was. We never forgot. So you are a fearless, ambitious girl –

She looks at Colette.

You remind me –

Colette I don't want to be a film star. I want –

Greta And it's the want I recognise, the want that is the same. Thank God I was lucky, this boy was born lucky.

Colette Which boy?

Greta You're looking at him. I got what I deserved. Only men succeed that way. I was lucky as a man is lucky. Remember that, or you can forget ambition.

Colette goes to take the tray out.

I notice you do not curtsey. I have a friend – a French friend – who maintains it is one of the tragedies of the twentieth century – the decline, indeed, the near disappearance of the curtsey.

Colette Hasn't your friend little to worry herself about?

Matthew enters, carrying a sketchbook.

Good day to you, Sir Matthew.

Matthew And the top of the morning to you, Colette.

Colette I'll see to your bath, madam, and I'll be leaving these dishes out on the lawn for the leprechauns to lick clean.

Greta Colette is cross with me – I was lamenting the decline of the curtsey. When I stay with the Rothschilds in Paris – it is sweet how the servants instinctively do so in the presence of royalty and their social superiors.

Colette I'm an Irishwoman. I have no social superiors.

Colette exits with the tray.

Matthew Who does she think she is?

Greta Joan Crawford.

Matthew That girl is an enigma. Like all women – a complete enigma. And none more so, of course, than yourself, my dearest Greta – tell me, how did you sleep?

Greta Tolerably. The peacock kept me company, but I am not complaining.

Matthew And breakfast – tolerable?

Greta I ate a little. I must – I must have my bath.

Matthew We've made plans for today. Show you Ireland in all its splendour. See could you take to it.

Greta Matthew, you have been kind enough to fly me to Europe – paid for me to travel – I never look a gift horse in the mouth, so here am I, stopping with you before I hit Paris, and now I must ask you – why did you invite me?

Matthew Do you remember my last exhibition in London? You were persuaded to see a private viewing.

Greta I do remember the paintings.

Matthew You told me those bogs and fields, the cliffs and the ocean – they had quite possessed me. You said perhaps you could live here – away from the world, halfway between New York and Sweden, where no one knew you.

Greta Did I say so much? Was I drunk?

Matthew Sober as a judge, but you did reveal you'd love to see my little house. I never forgot that. Fate made me ring you just when you were thinking of hitting Europe. What better time to stop and let me entertain you in my simple abode? I adore people staying – and it's been years since you last set eyes on my work. But I did save some of the paintings you admired. And look at this, I've been sketching. Would you care to take a peep?

He opens the sketchbook and shows her some pages.

Rough fumblings – the lake, we'll picnic there – Harry – what do you make of the likeness? Be brutal – they're hasty, but I think I'm improving with age. I have some juicy commissions in the offing. Say nothing, but a certain member of a certain family known to you, known to me – it's rumoured this grand lady – very grand lady – wants to sit for a portrait.

Greta The Queen Mother, is it?

Matthew I drop no names, but you are quite the detective, Miss Greta Garbo. How did you guess?

Greta From the way you are salivating, Sir Matthew. Have you asked her to sit here?

Matthew In this house – royalty? You are happily innocent of Irish history. We are only miles from the border dividing this island. We've called a truce between these nations. It may be 1967, but scratch these people slightly and there's still a hatred. You heard that girl. She's the rule, not the exception.

Greta has been leafing through the sketchbook.

Greta These are fine drawings – insofar as I know anything.

Matthew Too kind and too modest. Your taste in art is excellent. Your Renoirs alone –

Greta You must see them some day. I bought them because I listened to advice. My one virtue is I can listen and learn. All my best directors said so when –

Matthew But do you like the drawings?

Greta This Harry is a handsome man.

Matthew I may have softened him in this profile – isn't it strange? An old bugger like myself, I've always been keener on the ladies when it comes to my trade. Look at you, sitting in the passing blaze of a Donegal summer, surrounded by nothing but the radiance of sunlight – the way it makes you what you are. Garbo. The great Garbo. What I would give to paint you.

Greta hands him back the sketchbook.

Greta But first you must see to the Queen Mother. And I must see to my bath. I know I am safe from your wandering hands, Matthew, but I am not sure I trust your prying eyes. Be gone, and let me get ready to bathe.

Matthew I will see to it myself that the water is perfect. Let me give you this gift of a drawing.

Greta Please don't. It would embarrass me. I dislike gifts. And I have brought you so little. Here, let me find it –

Matthew I value anything from your fair hands.

She holds him a box of four chocolates from the pocket of her dressing gown.

Greta They gave this to us on the plane – I cannot eat much chocolate.

Matthew Still intact – all four – I shall treasure them.

He tears a drawing from the sketchbook and gives it to her, bowing.

A small thing, but my own. Dispose of it as you please. I shall not complain if I do not see it gracing the walls of your New York apartment.

Matthew exits, leaving Greta looking at the drawing.

Greta Ah, Matthew, word gets out I collect you, prices multiply.

She laughs.
Paulie enters.

Paulie Come in and soak yourself in the warm bath – I can heat no more water. Let me feel your hair – is it still damp?

Paulie touches Greta's hair.

I told you – the sun's done its job.

Greta Yes, and what is it you say in English?

Greta touches her own hair.

Bone dry. And now I must mind you. You must never stay out too long in the sun. It will damage your lovely skin – so clean. We must make sure you cover well these lovely cheeks. Those bones. Dry bones, beautiful.

She touches Paulie's face.

But why do I give you advice? You know already. How wise you are. And reliable.

She goes into the house as the peacock screeches.

Paulie Ever reliable. Always and ever reliable. Or I like to think so.

The peacock shrieks.

Act Two

SCENE ONE

The picnic beside the lake.
  Most of the food has been consumed.
  Plates and cutlery are nearly all cleared away back into the hamper.
  There are empty bottles of alcohol stacked aside, but some are still full or nearly so.
  Paulie and Sylvia are finishing the clean-up.
  James lies on his back, a glass in his hand.

James Where's my daughter?

Paulie Her and Harry must have walked on ahead. I cannot spot them. The trees must be hiding them.

James You should have stopped them going off together. Paulie? Pour.

He points to the empty glass.

Paulie Have you not had enough, James?

James It's free, isn't it? It's rare enough himself acts the big shot. Pour generously.

She does so.

Sylvia Why worry about Colette? You're surely not nervous of Harry molesting her?

James Harry's not all he seems – trust me. He'll line his pockets and do a runner from Sir Matthew. That boy is not as queer as he makes out. They never are. They still like to satisfy the ladies.

Sylvia You would know about satisfying ladies.

43

James Pour her more drink – with luck she'll pass out.

Paulie So far this afternoon we've watched ourselves well –

James Correction, sister, you've watched us well.

Paulie Don't spoil this lovely day – don't give the strangers that satisfaction. This picnic, it's bringing back such beautiful memories. As children, we had so many lovely meals on this spot.

James
'Jelly on the plate –
Jelly on the plate –'

Paulie A greengage jelly.

James
'Turn it over –
Turn it over –'

Paulie Mrs McFeely, our cook, was terrified of our father. We all were. The whole town feared his quick temper.

Sylvia Much good it did the old spendthrift. He died destitute. He left us nothing.

Paulie We have the house.

Sylvia Had. Didn't Sir Matthew buy you out lock, stock and barrel? And he lets you stay.

Sylvia laughs.

Paulie Sylvia, drink always brings out the best in your breed. You might do us all – yourself especially – an enormous favour. Go home. Go home now.

Sylvia No. I have to entertain the great film star, Greta Garbo. She is the woman I would have loved to be, though she hates me.

44

Paulie She cares for nobody enough to hate them – no more than she could love them. The woman is ice, cold as ice, warm as ice. She passes through our world, and we do not register, and that is what she gives us. It is in its strange way a kindness, for there is no pretence with her. What you see is what you get – Garbo. That has to be enough.

Sylvia And you know all that from a few days spent with her? How?

Paulie She tells me, and I listen.

Sylvia God, aren't you very smart? It's an awful pity you didn't get an education.

James Our parents didn't believe in education. For boys or for girls. I was barely let finish primary school. Reading a book – never. As for Paulie –

Paulie I am well able to read. I am well able to write my name. Never you say otherwise.

Her fierceness silences them.

My parents were clever people. They passed on their brains to both of us. The proof of the pudding is Colette. She will soon receive her Leaving Certificate results and we will see who will have the last laugh.

James I hope you're right.

Sylvia Here she comes with Harry.

James Why are they linked arm in arm?

Sylvia Let her have her dream, for Jesus sake. She won't get much mileage out of him, no matter what you imagine.

Colette and Harry enter.

45

Paulie That must have been a good dander. Are the other two after you?

Colette They're following – she has some energy, the old one.

Paulie Don't refer to anyone in that way. You'll be ancient yourself one day – if you're lucky.

Harry Colette's right. She's practically carrying Matthew. He can't keep up with her.

Colette Harry, will you come down with me to the school to collect my exam results?

James Why do you want him to accompany you?

Colette Because I'm going to faint and I want a big strong man to carry me home. And I want the other girls to be mad jealous – me arriving with Harry. They're all panting after him – I have them convinced he's my bars.

Harry I'm your what?

Paulie Her bars – Buncrana talk. It means her boyfriend.

Sylvia We have that expression in Derry as well. You look wonderful today, Harry. Very swanky, that shirt, lovely fit. I wish you were my bars as well.

James You'd think a girl intending to go to university would not sink to be talking in the language of the gutter.

Colette I'm not using dirty language. I just said –

James I heard what you said and I don't want you repeating it.

Colette How many has he had? Easy seeing someone's pouring the drink for nothing – getting a bit cross, are you? Always the way when you're half cut.

Paulie Colette, apologise to your father.

Colette What for?

Paulie I said, apologise.

Sylvia You heard your aunt – apologise.

Colette Three against one – is that it? I'll soon have nothing more to do with any of you – and won't I be happy then to be rid of you all?

Harry Don't be so damned cruel. Don't be such a spoilt child –

Colette I am spoilt, am I?

Harry You think the world adores you. Good for you, enjoy it while it lasts. Because it won't. You never know when the killer punch is coming, but it does, and there's no preparing for it.

Colette When did you turn into the good philosopher?

James Likely when he puts on his swanky shirt – a beautiful fit, isn't that what my wife said in her description? Jesus, Harry, my women are tripping over themselves to shower you with compliments. Here's the boss and his fancy woman. Watch out. All hands on best behaviour now. Paulie has issued her ultimatum – no shenanigans in front of the stranger.

Paulie And I mean it, James.

James I know you did, Paulie. That's why I'm repeating your warning. Listen to me butter her up when she arrives. Ten out of ten for my perfect manners.

Greta and Matthew enter, Matthew carrying a bottle of champagne.

Miss Garbo, I trust you enjoyed your stroll. We've missed your company.

47

Greta looks directly at him.

Something I was just remarking to the company. Your English is excellent. Did you learn it in Sweden?

Greta I am still learning it. I am still a beginner, in some respects.

James What respects would that be?

Greta Lying. I do find that remarkably difficult. Yes, I envy the ease with which it comes –

Sylvia To the English?

Greta To you all. It is perplexing.

Paulie Are you telling me you never tell lies, Miss Garbo?

Greta Matthew, how long have you known me? So many years since we stumbled across each other in the States – would you say that I lie?

Matthew Good God, I've never realised it – you don't lie. Why not?

Greta To save time. Matthew, you promised me a glass of cold champagne.

Matthew I've plucked it from the lake specially for you.

Greta I am quite parched. A glass of champagne, please.

Matthew Harry, will you do the honours?

> *Harry opens the champagne to applause and cheers.*
> *Paulie and Sylvia have been handing out glasses.*
> *James refuses, Colette is too young.*
> *Harry measures out five glasses of champagne.*
> *Paulie serves.*
> *As Harry opens the champagne and Paulie serves,*
> *Greta grows expansive.*

Greta But this is what I should have brought you – champagne. It just did not occur to me. You are so impossible to buy for, Matthew – you have so much. What do you give the man who has everything?

Sylvia A zebra.

They look at her.

James Where did I dig that woman out of?

Sylvia He doesn't have everything – do you see a zebra?

James My friends, this is what I live with – meet the zebra.

Sylvia I'm only pointing out he doesn't have everything. That's all I'm saying. So she got it wrong. Completely wrong. Totally wrong. Didn't you, Miss Greta Garbo? Cheers.

Matthew Sylvia, you are one of the few that drink compliments. The blush of wine is becoming on you. You should dress in matching colour to your cheeks. Plum – or better still, beetroot. Something that goes well with vinegar.

Sylvia I'll take that as flattery, whatever way it's intended. It's what was offered to Our Lord lying dying on the cross, poor Jesus – vinegar.

James So you would have shared a slug of it with him?

Sylvia Don't be disrespectful. I would have been standing weeping on Calvary there arm in arm with the Blessed Virgin, planning how we'd spend the rest of our days in Heaven, looking down on the sinners burning in Hell, gasping for a drop of water to cool their stinging tongues.

She raises her glass to Greta and Matthew.

Cheers.

Colette Miss Garbo, isn't there a village in Sweden called Hell?

Sylvia That's because everyone in Sweden's going to Hell – fuck them.

Paulie That's enough, thank you. Can we change the subject, please?

James I'll help myself instead to a wee dram. Anyone object? I hope not, for I'm going to do it anyway.

He has a large whiskey.

So, tell me, Miss Garbo, what do you make of us? What are your thoughts on Ireland?

Greta What do I know? I am a stranger. You tell me, what are your thoughts on Ireland?

James It is unfree, and Ireland unfree –

Greta How is it unfree?

James The British occupation across the border. That has to end, and it will end, for there is a change coming, a big one. There's a war brewing, mark my words –

Paulie Be quiet, James.

Sylvia Don't mock his patriotism.

James There has to be a war, because Ireland is unfree, and Ireland – unfree – will never be at peace.

Greta As you are not at peace.

There is a silence.

Well, aren't you? You are not at peace.

James This sedates me. After a dose of drink, the blood's not boiling.

He raises his glass.

Ireland sober is Ireland free. Cheers.

He sips the whiskey with relish.

Fuck freedom.

Matthew Dear James, so reliable. I hope he does not frighten you, Greta. He put the wind up Harry when he first arrived. Didn't he, my dear?

Harry I can't remember.

Matthew I can. You were quite convinced this wild man on the booze would murder us in our bed – English and queer, what hope had we?

James Abandon hope, all ye who enter here. That's Harry's motto, isn't it? Oops, sorry, speaking out of line.

Paulie Way out of line.

Sylvia Can we not just enjoy ourselves? None of this drunken –

James Yes, indeed, I should be quiet – I should just toddle off, on my way like a good lad – touch the forelock to Sir Matthew and let him pat my hair –

He affects an English accent.

Be off with you, my good man, and sin no more. We all know, yes, about sin –

Greta I have a problem understanding you. Did you say sin or sing?

James No picnic is complete without a song. Miss Garbo, our wonderful guest, in her delightful way, asks us, the people of this accursed isle, to entertain her –

Paulie Enough, James –

James She requests a song –

Sylvia Did you not hear your sister? Hit the road, boyo.

James bursts into song, singing 'Hit the Road, Jack'. He looks about him.

James No takers? Nobody else like Ray Charles? Dear old Ray Charles.

Sylvia rapidly breaks into the song 'Shall My Soul Pass Through Old Ireland?'

Sylvia
'In a dreary Brixton prison
Where an Irish soldier lay
By his side a priest was standing
Ere his soul should pass away.
And he faintly murmured, "Father,"
As he grasped him by the hand –

James and Paulie join in to make a trio.

Trio
"But tell me this before I die.
Shall my soul pass through Ireland?
But tell me this before I die,
Shall my soul pass through Ireland?"'

The song finishes and Paulie, James and Sylvia look at each other.

Greta Excellent – good voices – I did enjoy that, thank you.

Matthew Thank you, indeed. Wasn't it well sung, Harry?

James Very well sung, wouldn't you say so, Harry? No? Cat got your tongue? Struck dumb. Deaf, dumb and blind. Blind as dear old Ray Charles, to whom I return. Do you like Ray Charles, daughter dear?

Colette I don't know his music, Daddy.

James Head too full of the Beatles, Miss Garbo. They've lasted a bit – I thought they'd be dead and buried by now.

Colette I'm saving to buy *Sergeant Pepper's Lonely Hearts Club Band*.

James What's that when it's at home?

Colette The Beatles' new LP. It's supposed to be utterly brilliant – they played it all on Radio Luxembourg one night.

James Then sing us a song from it if it's that utterly brilliant.

Colette I can't sing and I don't have it yet.

James Then we'll have to rectify that. How much would it set you back? Would two pound cover it?

Sylvia Where did you get that extra two pounds?

Colette I'm saving for it, Daddy.

James But you want this Beatles thing – this lonely hearts? Don't we all, Miss Garbo? I can't see Colette go without. Can you, Sylvia?

Paulie She's asking where you got the money?

Sylvia Are you going to answer me?

James Why the suspicion?

There is a silence.

I see – old memories. The police won't come calling – no worries, girls. Skittering two pound. I backed a horse. Catherine Wheel. One shilling each way. Came in at 33–1. So I cleared two pounds for my two shillings. Satisfied? Check the bookies if you like.

Sylvia I might.

James You do. But anyway, here it is, and I am giving it to my only daughter to celebrate St Patrick's Day.

Paulie James, this isn't March 17th, we're in the middle of August.

James Just checking, Paulie. See if you're still as sharp as ever. This sister of mine – the family historian, Miss Garbo, great with dates. Never forgets. A walking calendar girl.

He sings.

'I love – I love my little calendar girl.'

Who sang that, Sylvia?

Sylvia Neil Sedaka.

James Your old favourite. No worries back then, eh?

Sylvia nods.

Let me give her the money. Take it, pet, take.

He hands Colette the two pounds.

Buy what you like. Neil Sedaka – no, he must be long forgotten. Get your Beatles record.

Sylvia Neil Sedaka will never be forgotten, James.

Colette Thanks, Da.

James Never say thanks for money. Take the hand off those giving it. The only way to live. I wish you were buying Ray Charles though. Jesus, but I love him singing.

He bursts into song.

'I can't stop loving you – it's useless to say.'

He stops.

Funny – can remember no more of that. Gone right out of my head. Can't sing the blues. Only the blacks can. They're the only ones can box as well. Did you fight any black men in your day, Harry? Did you knock a few of them into the middle of next week when you were fit and up for it?

Harry I fought a few.

James And were they tough? Did they send you spinning? Did your arse feel the ground through its silk shorts?

Harry My arse can look after itself, James.

Greta A Swede was heavyweight champion of the world. Ingemar Johansson. World champion. We were all very proud of him. Did you fight him, Harry?

Harry He was out of my league, Miss Garbo. But you were right to be proud of him. A gentleman, I'm told, and a fine boxer.

James Who told you he was a gentleman?

Harry That was the word.

James Where?

Harry In the sport.

James Irishmen – take on any Irishmen?

James takes up a boxing pose.

Could I take you on? What would you do if I stepped up –

Harry I'd run away, James – that's what fighters are trained to do.

Matthew Gentlemen, no fisticuffs – ladies present.

James Our guest enjoys watching a good hiding, no? Up Ingemar – up Sweden.

55

Greta I do not get involved in fights.

James Let others battle, smart woman. Come on, Harry, take me on –

Paulie I'm tempted to take the eejit on myself, Harry, but spare him the lesson he's looking for.

[handwritten annotation: Irish for idiot]

James Come on, cissy boy, fight me.

Sylvia Flatten the fucker, Harry.

Harry Your wish is my command.

Colette Stop it, Daddy.

> *Harry makes a playful move on James.*
> *James tries to throw a punch.*
> *Harry skilfully dodges it.*

Stop it, Harry.

> *Harry goes to land a serious blow on James.*
> *James suddenly freezes.*
> *Harry grabs him in a bear hug.*

Harry I quite like being a cissy, James.

> *Harry kisses James on the mouth.*
> *Sylvia bursts out laughing.*
> *She sees the look on the others' faces, especially Harry's, and stops.*
> *Harry does not release James from the bear hug and whispers in his ear.*

Don't every try to be fucking smart with me, Irish, for if I choose, I will kill you. Remember that.

> *Harry lets James go.*

Sylvia At least there's one man about the house.

> *James goes to put on his jacket.*

Colette Are you all right, Daddy?

Sylvia Answer your daughter. Have you not got your breath back? You're not as full of big chat now, are you? Why don't you answer me? Why are you staring into space? What are you looking at?

James The lake where I was reared by – that's what I'm looking at. Someday I'll walk into it, and I will not walk out.

Sylvia Don't threaten me with that old buck, James. I don't believe you – I've heard that too many times. I've seen you walk back through the front door too often.

James calmly produces a gun from his jacket pocket.

James Have you seen this too often?

Sylvia Fire it, you fucker, fire it.

James Where, Sylvia? At you? Waste of a good bullet. At the Englishmen? Do myself out of a job. At myself? I've been told I'd never be man enough. So where do I fire it? Any suggestions?

Greta Into space where you were staring. Into the stars. Into the blue sky.

James That is what I will do. I will shoot God and his angels. He can put an end to me for this misdeed. Watch – learn – listen.

He aims the gun into the sky and it goes off.

Fuck me, it's loaded – the gun's loaded. I've been carrying that about with me in my good jacket pocket and it's loaded. Did you know this was loaded?

Sylvia Don't you know I would have used it if I did?

James Who in hell put the ammunition in it? Paulie, who –

Paulie It must have been like that since the War of Independence –

James Nearly fifty years ago – and it's still live. Wait until I tell the boys in the Drift Inn about this – wait until I tell them –

He charges off, still delighted.

They'll stand me a fair few rounds. I'll have to show them the gun – do you think there's more in her?

He fires the gun at Sylvia as he exits.

Empty.

He stops and looks around at the others.

Just as well, eh?

James is gone.

Sylvia Colette, I need to follow your daddy – come with me. A kind good evening to you all.

Colette and Sylvia exit. There is an uneasy silence.

Paulie Never a dull moment, at least.

Matthew Are there any more live guns here, Paulie?

Paulie I wouldn't know.

Matthew A worrying development, don't you think?

Paulie We all know he's harmless. I'll have a word with him when he's sober.

Matthew No – this time I might.

Paulie Oh dear, a warning?

Matthew An emperor never warns, Rasputin – he commands. And my wish –

He turns to Harry.

What is my wish, Harry?

Harry Tell me, Matt.

Matthew I wish to go for a stroll. Come with me. Get rid of that gun. We have to save your brother from himself, Paulie. And we also have to save ourselves. Greta, may we escort you back to the house?

Greta No, I will wait here a little. I want to see if God falls out of the sky – is James that good a shot? I will see you there.

Matthew and Harry exit as Paulie starts to clean up glasses, pouring what remains of the champagne into Greta's glass.

Paulie You can say you've now seen us in our full glory.

Greta I rarely notice things.

Paulie It would be hard not to observe that James is fond of the bottle.

Greta As is his lady wife.

Paulie But they can still do their work. Never a scratch on the car – never the smallest accident in all his years driving –

Greta A clean record – a model citizen –

Paulie I wouldn't go that far –

Greta Still, you protect him, because he is your beloved flesh and blood. Women do.

Paulie I suppose so. Still, I feel obliged to you for understanding –

Greta Him – her – his wife – his daughter – I understand.

Paulie Still, a wee bit of a shock to strangers, our ones.

Greta Why? You have made me particularly welcome. Firing a gun in my honour. Who would have believed that turn of events? I come to Ireland and find myself in a cowboy picture. My first western. I presume this shooting, or something similar, happens each week?

Paulie Christ above, no – I'm telling you the truth –

Greta I know you do. Just as well. I recognise lies instantly.

Paulie Then you'll be a busy woman if you stay in Ireland. We're all liars –

Greta James asked me what did I make of Ireland? Shall I tell you?

Paulie I'm all ears.

Greta You give away all your secrets. You shouldn't do that when there are strangers present. They might believe you. Best to leave them guessing – that's what I find. Of course, I may be mistaken – very mistaken. It has happened before, but I never admit it. I never admit anything. Then neither do you, do you?

> *Greta exits, handing Paulie the glass of champagne.*
> *Paulie stands holding the glass.*
> *The peacock shrieks.*

Act Three

SCENE ONE

The kitchen.
    It is morning a few days later.
    Paulie breaks eggs and beats them. There are some herbs beside the bowl that she chops in the course of the scene and adds to the eggs.
    Greta enters.

Paulie You missed all the excitement.

Greta I do try to always. I went out walking –

Paulie Without breaking your fast?

Greta A sturdy walk is better for the body than breakfast. If you do not exercise, you will catch a disease and die.

Paulie I'll bear that in mind. As I said, you missed the excitement. Colette's results have arrived –

Greta Results? Is she ill? Is it medical tests –

Paulie Do you ever listen to us? Her exam results. She's passed. She's more than passed. Excelled herself. Even better than she was hoping. The nuns who taught her are dancing. She's down in the convent to see them. Their star pupil, off to university.

Greta She has got what she sought?

Paulie Sought? More even.

Greta And she shares her success with her friends?

Paulie Jesus, would you believe this, I don't think Colette has any friends.

Greta She will not fear jealousy then – I am glad for her.

Paulie So you approve of loneliness?

Greta I made a career out of it. Haven't you heard?

Paulie I never believe what I hear.

Greta So you trust no one? It's why you never married? Why you are like me – an old bachelor?

Paulie In this country it's called being an old maid.

Greta I prefer bachelor. It is braver somehow. And in New York I am celebrated as one of the city's most confirmed bachelors – myself and Cardinal Spellman.

Paulie Something I'm dying to ask you, but you must be exhausted answering it.

Greta I am always exhausted – I always have been. It impresses people.

Paulie Why exactly did you stop making films?

Greta Tragedies should be borne without complaint.

Paulie Why was it a tragedy? You just stopped –

Greta For once I must be brave – be manly. I must walk away. And I did. But I was always a strange child. That is why I must mind myself always. You mind others – your family, your house. To me that would be hell –

Paulie I don't mind hell –

Greta Neither do I, provided it is of my choosing. And in that respect we are alike. I say that to so few people, but you I can trust. Do you know why?

Paulie shakes her head.

When we were born, we both looked like boys.

62

Paulie But I turned into a woman. I am female –

Greta That is a beautiful quality. I may not have very much of it.

Paulie You were the most beautiful –

Greta Woman in the world. And when I looked in the mirror I always saw my father.

Paulie He looked like –

Greta Like your brother. Drunk, always drunk.

Paulie And your mother –

Greta She married my father. She lived with him. She let him drink. I was the drunkard's daughter. Taking me on long, lonely walks, teaching me all he knew about the earth, walking me to exhaustion that I have never shaken out of my Viking bones. My great, tall giant of a father. Karl Alfred Gustaffson. Looking up at him, my brother, myself, my sister Alva. My dead sister – dancing on the table. My kind, my gentle, my only sister – taken from me. A man did it, a cruel man. She died young. It was the sorrow of my life. My face knew it. No more secrets – I could not hide in front of the camera. It did not forgive me mourning in grief for my dear, dead, dancing sister.

Paulie You danced on the table?

Greta Our kitchen table – the tango, the waltz –

Paulie climbs onto the table.

What are you doing?

Paulie Would you care to join me?

Greta laughs.

Greta Dear me, Garbo laughs – once it made headlines.

Paulie I asked, would you join me? Are you refusing a sad old bachelor?

Greta We will fall off the table – I have no head for heights.

Paulie I do as you bid me. I'll come down to dance with you.

Greta gives Paulie a hand to get down from the table. Still holding Greta's hand, Paulie asks:

Tell me this, lassie, do you tango?

Greta Not for many years.

Paulie I hear the Pope doesn't approve of it. Or Cardinal Spellman.

Greta Then shall we dance?

*Making their own music, Paulie and Greta tango.
At its end, they fall into each other's arms, laughing till Paulie pulls away as Matthew enters the library to consult a book.*

Paulie Jesus Christ, years since I danced.

Greta Why did you stop?

There is a short silence.

Why are you sad?

Paulie Like yourself, I'm exhausted.

Greta What has exhausted you?

Paulie I lost control once.

Greta Dancing?

Paulie No – not dancing. It happened when I had to emigrate – we'd lost the lot, the family business. Left destitute. James went to work on the roads of England.

Not fit for it. His letters home would have broken your heart. Me, I went to a factory in Scotland. I was timid as a child hearing the orders barked at me, trying my best to follow them – me, who was always my own boss, reduced to this. First day on the floor – the gangs of strangers speaking in thick Scotch accents – I was so nervous. All the men with scars, even young women with tattoos. I wasn't brave enough to ask where the toilets were – the water ran down my legs – I wet – my legs. I lost control.

She laughs quietly.

The water ran down my wet – I've never told this to any stranger.

Greta There are some things – about the human body – one shouldn't talk about or tell. No, I do not think you should say this to a stranger.

Paulie I'm sorry if I offend you –

Greta Yes, I accept you are, but I can say no more about it, for if I did, I too would lose control, and then people like you, strangers, would cease to look at me. You might start to look inside me, and I would dislike that.

Matthew enters the kitchen.

Matthew What is it you now dislike, Greta? What can I add to your long list of aversions?

Greta I do not think I shall tell you. You neglect me, you ignore me, you bring me to this strange place and then I am left utterly alone. Do you do this to all your guests?

Matthew I must work, my dear. You cannot fault me for that. Money must be earned. Greta, I don't live on my rents. We cannot all be ladies of leisure, gallivanting around the globe.

Greta I do not gallivant. I travel with a purpose.

Paulie What was your purpose coming here – pure badness?

Matthew Greta came here because I invited her.

Greta And I was intrigued.

Paulie By what?

Greta To be so far north – this is as far north as I can be in Ireland, isn't it? There are times I only want to live where there is nothing but the sea and the land ending. One more step, and we can flee from the earth. Go back and live where we started. We would be happier than we are now – better people, in the ocean where we belong – in the deep water – that is really my home. I am haunted by it – I am haunted by the sea. Matthew, have James drive me back to see the Atlantic – I love looking at it.

Matthew Then do as I've been asking you –

Greta Plaguing me, but I cannot –

Matthew Buy this house. You're safe here. No one knows you in these parts – no threat from those damned snappers with their cameras, hounding. There's just the lake – and it's really a fjord, honestly. It really is just like Sweden. Perfect for you, Greta. And the price is insanely cheap. I'll even throw in a portrait of your good self. What do you say? Do we have a deal?

Greta I buy your house, and you paint my portrait? But what shall happen to you? Homeless, reputation ruined, seeing this old lady as your latest masterwork.

Matthew It would be a pleasure and a privilege –

Greta You are too kind.

Matthew The kindness is all yours.

Greta I am never kind, Matthew. To be so, I would need a heart that gives all and sundry whatever it is they ask for. People ask too much, so that they can be satisfied, but God has denied me such a heart.

Matthew So you turn down my offer?

Greta Why do you want to leave here?

Matthew Too comfortable – turning into family. I dislike family.

Paulie What would Harry make of this?

Matthew I'm sure you're worried about him – it is not his house. And you really shouldn't be listening, Paulie.

Paulie What am I? The invisible woman?

Matthew Invisibility – the highest aspiration of the Victorian servant.

Paulie Victoria is dead and buried and I'd dance on her grave.

Matthew But you have too much control to do that, don't you, Paulie? Wonderful control. A sturdy pair of kidneys. Am I right? You can say nothing in this place. Everybody hears everything. It's why I want rid of it.

Colette races in, followed by James and Sylvia.

Paulie Stop charging about the place – you'll knock someone down.

Matthew Is there any sign of rain?

Colette beams at both Matthew and Greta.

Colette It's really a beautiful day – the sun will shine for sure.

Matthew Greta, shall we risk a walk?

67

Greta No, I have had my walk – I must rest a little. And you must paint. Work – work, my dear. It is your way. Paint the peacock – that I'd like to see.

Matthew Is that a commission?

Greta It is an order, and gentlemen always follow orders, don't they, Miss Hennessy?

She gives her arm to Matthew, and they exit together. Colette, still smiling, follows them and watches them leave.

Colette Did you not say anything to them? I mean, you'd think they might offer congratulations – well done – something.

Paulie But they didn't. How are the proud parents? You must be delighted. Why are your faces like long?

James She has our heads turned.

Sylvia All this talk about traipsing off to Dublin.

James She's done well.

Paulie No denying that. The best in Donegal. Maybe even the best in Ulster. The nuns are finding out if she's got top marks in Ireland –

Colette Wouldn't that be mighty?

Paulie It would be in all the papers.

Sylvia Are you that anxious to get our names again in the papers?

James Are you dragging this up once more?

Sylvia We might have had our fill of them.

James Will you never tire –?

Sylvia Nobody in this town ever tires of upcasting it to me – the night you lifted a purse –

James I found it, with a miserable ten-shilling note.

Sylvia You stole it. And yet you deny doing so. It has to go to court because of that. Buncrana man found guilty of theft. Whatever hope we had of recovery – that was out the window. Thieves and liars – didn't I do well marrying into this breed? The same ones who would have slammed their door shut on my like –

James If you hadn't got your foot firmly inside it. And once you'd perched your arse in our kitchen, you made damned sure it wouldn't be kicked out.

Sylvia grabs Colette.

Sylvia Is she what you're referring to? Take a good look, mister. This one is yours and mine. Sorry to disappoint you – I dropped only one child, and Colette is yours.

Colette Jesus, will I be glad to get rid of yous all.

Sylvia Will you – will you be glad? Well, put a stop to your gladness. You're not going.

Colette What do you mean?

Sylvia Jesus, I'm sorry – I thought you spoke all different languages. Did you not get the best marks in Ireland for them? Maybe I'm wrong – maybe I'm thick – is English not one of them? Did you not understand what I said loud and clear? You're not going to Dublin. Ask your father why.

Paulie You cannot stop her. Why can she not go to university?

James We haven't the money.

Colette I'll win a scholarship – I'm bound to –

James It's not enough, pet. It barely covers the digs and books. What will you live on?

Colette Fresh air. I will starve –

James For seven years? That's what medicine takes. And the extras involved, all the ins and the outs – the cost is criminal.

Sylvia It's not for people our like.

Paulie Who's given you all this inside knowledge?

Sylvia He went down this morning to Dr McSharry – he kindly explained all –

Paulie McSharry is a soak who should have been struck off years ago. What did our local butcher of a medicine man explain precisely – what did he in his wisdom advise?

James Teaching – she should go into some class of teaching. Qualify in two or three years. Earn a good wage. Help her mother and father.

Sylvia Pay back what they've done for her.

James She could study for that nearer home – in Derry, or at the new university in Coleraine. Whatever way you look at it, teaching is a good job. Never get your hands dirty, girl. You'll always get work. You might not even need to go to get a degree. There's other qualifications –

Colette That Dr McSharry wouldn't clean his arse with.

Sylvia You have a bit of respect for –

Colette Respect? That word comes out of your mouth, mother? What are you? Stupid and ignorant – a dead loss, to me, to him, to yourself.

Sylvia James, slap her across the face.

Paulie If he does, he'll feel mine –

Sylvia For once in your life, stay out of our business.

Have you not always done us more than enough harm? What did I tell you this morning, James? This is a battle that should have been fought in our own house.

Colette How long have you known what I set my heart on? What I worked myself to the bone for? When you were patting yourselves on the back that I wasn't gadding about running to dances, did it not dawn on you how serious I was? Do you think I was passing the time –

Sylvia You weren't running to dances because you had nobody to run with. Nobody likes you, you don't let them. And if the girls think you're odd as two left feet, what must the fellows think of you?

Colette I care nothing for the fellows in this town – thick as poundies –

Sylvia Then keep on not caring. No matter how you end up – teacher or doctor – you'll still find yourself talking to the air in your lonely kitchen.

Paulie I think somehow I'm being used as a warning here, Colette. So, take stock of me, and then look at your mammy and daddy – the joys of marriage.

Colette I've been in the middle of these battles between the three of you too often. I'm not wasting my breath defending one or the other. Times have changed. I know what I'm doing – go to Dublin, to University College Dublin, study medicine –

James Will you not knuckle down to do Arts? It's only three years –

Colette Why did you let me dream I could do medicine? Jesus, Mammy, do you hate me that much you could put a stop –

Sylvia Do you think I'm doing this out of hate?

Colette Why else are you putting him up to it? Don't say you're not. You're always the ringmaster, and he follows you. Why do this to me if it is not hate?

Sylvia Because I don't want you to leave me. Because I don't know what's going to happen to you, far away from home. I don't want you to go. Don't leave me, Colette. Please don't leave me.

Colette I have to go.

Sylvia Why?

She does not answer. Greta enters the library, selecting a book, immersing herself in it.

If I'm on my own here, I'm lost.

Colette You're not on your own here.

Sylvia Who have I but you?

She points to James.

Him?

She points to Paulie.

Her? She aids and abets him. Two against one. Always. You are my only defence. Because you are right. I am stupid. I am ignorant. I am a dead loss. But I gave birth to you. I did something with my life. Something – one thing right. And I don't want to lose you.

Colette This is the way to lose me. Stop crying – please – I'm sorry –

Sylvia Why did we let you dream you could be a doctor? I'll tell you. We never thought you would qualify to enter medicine. What was it old McSharry more or less told your father? That's not for people our like. And why is it we agree, James? Your old saying –

James When the plate's full, it falls.

Paulie It hasn't fallen.

James It will, Paulie.

Paulie Then we'll do as we did before – piece it together again.

James Better off putting the lot in the bin. She has to learn, Paulie –

Colette Learn what?

James Life kicks you hard in the arse, lady. Learn to rough it. You've had it easy, my girl, very easy, too easy. You will not get what you want. You will not do medicine in Dublin. We cannot afford it and we will not borrow. Nobody would lend it any road. Settle for less. Your father has spoken.

Colette There's no point arguing?

James None.

Colette Then we'll wait and see. I'm going out to tell Harry my news. At least there's one man in this house who isn't a jealous bastard.

   Colette exits.

Paulie You played a blinder there, Jimmy.

James Did I?

Paulie An absolute blinder. You were in cracking form as well, Sylvia. Good to learn what you make of my family.

Sylvia I see, as usual, I'm not included in that –

Paulie Why should you want to be after what you said about our brood? Thieves and liars – why be tarred with that brush?

Sylvia I spoke in the heat of the moment.

Paulie You do, yes. Don't apologise. It's what I expect from the two of you. And you were right about the thief. But it was a lot more than a ten-shilling note. James, you robbed me – robbed me of my living – my happiness – my house. You'll do the same to your daughter as you did to your sister – and to your wife –

James I have made up my mind. I know what's best for my girl –

Paulie You destroyed us –

James She will follow her father's advice –

Paulie I will not let you get away with it this time –

James I got away with nothing – that's why I am where I am –

Paulie People think it's queers don't like women. I'm beginning to wonder.

James You're very fond of the nancy boys. I know why. Not just because they pay the wages, is it? You're as fucking bent as they are. Colette accuses me of being jealous. It's you who are jealous. You didn't get the hand down her first to corrupt her.

Paulie gives a cry of pain.

Sylvia Dear Christ, James – no, that is shameful.

James Let her cry her eyes out. You mean, mean dog, Paulie. I was the one carried you home like a corpse from Scotland. I was the one saw you were put where you could be cared for – locked in a hospital ward. That is our shame, you dirty, barren bitch.

There is a silence.
Paulie is suddenly, shockingly calm.

74

Paulie I cannot argue with that.

Sylvia He didn't mean it –

Paulie Can I, Sylvia?

Sylvia Forgive him, Paulie.

Paulie Colette will go to Dublin. She'll study Arts. I'll give her whatever savings I've pieced together. If it's the last thing I do, I'll send her to university. You will neither of you argue with me on that. You will agree to it, if I am ever to forgive you.

Sylvia You have to agree, James.

Paulie It's not me he tells. He'll give his word elsewhere. He'll make his vow at my parents' grave. They will hear him say it. I alone beside him – no outsiders.

Sylvia I'm his wife.

Paulie And you deserve him. You've heard my terms. Follow me this instant to where our father and our mother are buried. State your piece there, we'll shake on it, or I will never again break breath with you.

Paulie exits.

Sylvia Maybe you shouldn't go with her.

Silence.

Maybe this time we should call her bluff and not let her bully us.

Silence.

My advice is call her bluff and hold your ground. I mean, she says it was her house you lost, but it was ours more so – you were the only son. And she spent money like water, painting and papering it, best of furniture and ornaments – fancy clothes, hair done once a week – she helped ruin the business, thinking she was somebody.

James She was more than you ever were, or ever will be.

James exits.

Sylvia James, I don't think you should say that – you shouldn't go – you shouldn't follow her.

Greta enters the kitchen, unseen by Sylvia.

You should stay with me. Why will you not?

Greta Your life is hard. Very hard, Mother.

Sylvia Mother? Are you going to laugh at me? Go on, mock. I'll let you. It's all I'm worth. Break your hole laughing. It's all I've left to do. Laugh.

Greta Then you are brave.

Sylvia Brave as can be. Brave enough to tell you Paulie imagines you might buy this house. But you won't. I know what you'll do. Trip the light fantastic back to America. Get out – do a runner – do what we should have done as a young married couple – me and James. Leave this country.

Greta Why did you not?

Sylvia He did leave. Working on the roads in England. Living in digs that never saw a scrubbing brush – the very particular, well-reared Master James Hennessy, sharing rooms with lads he looked down his nose at all his life in this town, lads who it turned out were good to him. Back then was the only time he ever wrote me letters. I kept one.

Greta What does it say?

Sylvia opens her purse and takes out a faded piece of writing.

Sylvia 'Navvying is wild hard. I sleep my fill sound at night as soon as my head hits the pillow. I enclose a few

76

pound – more I hope maybe next week. The men are rough, no denying, but say nothing in case their people hear you for they welcomed me and helped me get a start. I am glad in a way I have to work my fingers to the bone for it stops me thinking of home. But of course I remember all the time you and Colette. I have to put your faces out of my mind. If I didn't, I would die.'

She folds the page back into her purse.

Greta What did you write back?

Sylvia 'Don't die, James. Come home.' And he did. And I lived with him. Do you know what I think we did wrong? I should have gone with him. The three of us might have made a fist of it together in England. I think there's still time to do that. Would you help us out? Get us a start in New York – in Hollywood – anywhere in the States. There must be millions of people looking for chauffeurs. James is the best driver. I'd leave any house shining like a new pin. Morning, noon and night we'd slave, given a chance. Do you know of anybody who'd need us? It would have to be together, for without me he'd fall apart. Can you help us do that?

Greta I do not have a car. I am satisfied with my maid. She does everything I need in my apartment.

Sylvia So there's no hope?

Silence.

Well, if you do buy the house, will you consider keeping us on?

Greta I will listen to Matthew's references.

Sylvia We serve him well – he shouldn't complain. And we come cheap. You can ask Paulie as well. She'll put in a good word, and not just because we're her own.

I would ask you don't remember most of this conversation. Continue to insult me if you like – not that I take anything seriously.

Greta I do.

Matthew enters.

Matthew Sylvia, here you are entertaining Miss Garbo. I must be selfish and borrow her for a short while on urgent business. Excuse us.

Sylvia You're not telling me to go, but my hat's in the hall. An old Derry saying for get out. I'll be on my way.

She exits.

Greta You are agitated, Matthew – why?

Matthew Greta, I do believe you have become my inspiration – my muse –

Greta I have been to many – all of them bored me. Will you?

Matthew I've started the painting. The peacock, as you asked. It's speeding along at a wonderful rate –

Greta Good. May I see it before I go, yes?

Matthew You're leaving? When?

Greta Tomorrow. I have come to a decision. I must act on it. No shilly-shallying. Thank you for your kindness, Matthew. Do fetch me that girl – Colette, is that her name? She seems intelligent – she can pack for me.

Matthew And the house?

Greta What about it?

Matthew Will you –?

Greta Buy it? Not without proper advice. I always need to think long and hard. I have enjoyed being here. Meeting you again. And the people who surround you. Quite a gang. They love you. They have made me feel like one of the family. You know how I feel about family.

Matthew No, in fact, I don't.

Greta Talking, talking, singing. What was it James sang that day of the picnic?

Greta sings.

'Hit the road, Jack, don't you come back no more –'

She looks at Matthew.

Yes, good advice – Jack will hit the road.

Greta exits, leaving Matthew alone.

SCENE TWO

A meadow by the lake.
Harry scythes long grass.
He sees Colette but continues working as he speaks.

Harry Christ, you look fit to be tied. Why the temper?

Colette They won't let me do medicine. All my work – a waste of time. They say they can't afford it – even with a scholarship.

Harry continues working.

It's not fair, Harry, is it?

Harry How can I help you?

Colette Sir Matthew. Ask him to lend me the money.

Harry bursts out laughing and stops working.

Harry I think you're serious, girlie.

Colette Are you telling me you've never touched him for a few pounds?

Harry If I have, and I'm not saying I have, that would be my business, and his business, not yours.

Colette Harry, please – I'm only coming out with this because I'm desperate. Don't turn your back on me – don't. You're my last hope.

Harry I'm not, Colette – I'm no hope. Even if you could change my mind on this, there would be no point my trying to get money out of Matt. You know that – blood from a stone, darling, blood –

Colette I'm not your darling.

Harry Nor am I yours, and ain't I the lucky guy?

Harry goes back working.

Colette Are you really, Harry, are you lucky? Do you never regret selling yourself short the way you have?

Harry goes on working.

Touched a sore spot, have I? Glad to see it – some sign of decency – some hope that somewhere inside there's the remains of a normal man.

Harry stops working.
He looks at Colette.
He raises the scythe.
He examines it carefully.

Harry Do you see this? What is it?

Colette An old scythe – that's all.

Harry Do you know how you can chop a man's head off with a scythe?

Colette shakes her head.

Lifted clean away, right from the shoulder?

She shakes her head.

They say it bounces when it falls off the body. Like a ball – all along the ground. But that depends on how accurate the blow is – the more accurate, the more precise, the more the head bounces. How precise do you think I would be? You've seen me cutting the grass. What would you guess? Very – not very – a little – not at all precise?

Colette I don't know.

Harry So you say, and that's the difference between you and Matthew. He knew I was very – very accurate – very precise. And do you know, he wasn't afraid? Do you think it was because he saw me?

Colette Saw you what?

Harry Take the head off a man's shoulders. That was when he decided – I must have that boy in my bed, I like the way he looks, the way he moves, but most of all I admire his accuracy in a fight. What do you say about that?

Colette does not speak.

I had to leave boxing – I was warned off. Do you know why? Too much blood on my hands, darling, just too much blood. Have you ever shaken hands with a killer?

Colette shakes her head.

Good – no blood on your hands. And no blood from a stone, as I've said before in answer to your begging. Will I ask Sir Matthew for money for you? No, I will not. Understand?

Colette Very clearly.

Harry goes back working.

You'll say nothing about what I asked you to do?

Harry Matt's heading this way. It's the first thing I'll tell him.

Colette Do that and I'll spill the beans to all and sundry that you killed a man.

Harry I can deny it. I can deny anything.

Matthew enters.

I always do.

Matthew What are you denying this young lady?

Harry Her heart's desire.

Colette God forgive you.

Harry She wanted a kiss from me – to celebrate her great success. She's passed her exams with flying colours. Round it off, the finishing touch.

Colette I asked for no kiss –

Matthew Well, hip-hip-hooray for the red, white and blue –

Colette Green, white and gold – this is Ireland. That's the colour of our flag –

Matthew I am never allowed to forget it. Run along to the house. Miss Garbo needs a hand to pack.

Harry She's leaving us?

Matthew For Paris.

Harry That's a bit sudden.

Matthew Not really. It's where she was going. We were nothing more that a stopover. Do run along and offer to help, my dear. I'm sure she'll tip you well.

Colette runs off.

But I wouldn't count on it. Miss Greta has a serious aversion to putting her hand in her trousers pocket. She's turned down my offer of the house. Such privacy here. She wants to be alone – well, your wish would be granted, Garbo. And when I ask – will she let me draw her profile? Only a drawing? An absolute refusal. Insufferable woman. Good riddance.

Harry You didn't mention anything to me.

Matthew Mention?

Harry The house – selling it.

Matthew Yes, I've kept that quiet.

Harry I think you might have said something.

Matthew What business to you is my selling my own house? I fail to understand why you might expect –

Harry It's me that fails, Matt. Fails to know why in fuck I stick it out with you.

Matthew Then don't, my dear. Back you go to dear old Blighty. Don't let me delay you. You must have other fish to fry. I do believe you're hungry for fish – for the smell of them, the taste of them – go on. Don't let me stop you feasting on fish.

Harry does not answer.

Did you not want to kiss her – that stupid little bitch?

Harry Christ, Matt, is this what you're sinking to? It's been a while since I listened to the rant against me and women. To be honest, it's beneath you.

Matthew Where you will never be – and where I am rarely.

Harry You rarely let me.

Silence.

Why do you not let me touch you?

Silence.

Matthew I do.

Harry Rarely.

Matthew I have to work. To paint.

Harry So hard?

Matthew I can never afford to stop.

Harry Even if it's only to take a rest –

Matthew I don't rest. You know that. I never rest.

Harry You sleep soundly enough.

Matthew That is not rest.

Harry I like looking at you when you sleep.

Harry holds Matthew's face in his hands.

Matthew Don't touch me. I dislike being touched.

He continues to hold Matthew's face.

How long will I endure you? How can I accept your revolting sympathy? Your appalling touch? I would be free of you – rid of you – if you would just fuck off, my sweet. Do me that blissful, enormous, liberating favour, Harry. Please fuck off.

Harry kisses Matthew's cheek.

Harry With pleasure. Where?

*p nn necessatio to
leave you)*

Matthew I leave that choice entirely up to you.

Harry Shall we fly to Paris with Miss Garbo?

Matthew We must leave the divine Greta to her next victims.

Harry Victims?

Matthew The woman is a vampire. She is positively Romanian. A duchess to Dracula. I am sorely tempted to drive a stake through her heart, if the Queen of Transylvania has a heart. No, we shall avoid Paris. Choose somewhere else to leave me.

Harry Nice to see London again.

Matthew London it shall be. There's a change coming to these dark parts. One thing I picked up from my stint in the army – I can smell when a scrap might get out of hand. Time to run, my dear. New money in London – new dealers. Time to introduce ourselves. Plans, work –

Harry You didn't ask why exactly Colette was talking to me.

Matthew I have no interest in knowing why.

Harry She wants to be a doctor. Her family can't afford it.

Matthew That is tragic. Why should this concern you or me?

Harry Will you give her the money?

Matthew She asked you to ask me that?

Harry She did. Will you?

Matthew considers this.

Matthew No.

Harry Why?

Matthew God will provide. Wash before dinner. You smell, my sweet. I may ravish you.

Matthew exits, leaving Harry looking after him.
Harry shrugs and starts working again, brandishing the scythe.

SCENE THREE

The kitchen.
Greta examines her packed suitcase, the flowered scarf in her hand.
Colette stands at a distance from her.

Greta Excellent. You have followed my instructions perfectly.

Colette I did as you told me.

Greta This is how I like my suitcase to be packed. Everything is precisely where it should be. It is why I travel so lightly. A few cashmere sweaters – a few pairs of slacks – nothing too extravagant. You would think it should be the easiest thing in the world to get right, but no – the mess people can make. I do believe they take delight in throwing another person's belongings together any which way. But you – you certainly know how to care for a lady's clothes and how to pack a suitcase.

Colette Thank you.

Greta If you ever need a reference as a maid – even a lady's maid – I will be glad to oblige. I have my own reliable girl – they call them girls in America no matter what age. Otherwise I might be tempted to steal you away and smuggle you with me into New York.

Colette I wouldn't fit in your luggage. It's too tightly packed.

Greta Yes, it is – it is. No, you wouldn't fit indeed. Very amusing. But tell me, we have time to pass, do you intend to follow your family's example and go into domestic service?

Colette I thought I'd told you I had other ambitions.

Greta My dear, I am growing older – I forget. Remind me again – what are they?

Colette It's all right you forgetting. I've changed my mind what I want to do.

Greta You are a smart girl, aren't you?

Colette I used to think so.

Greta You do not like marriage, do you?

Colette I hate it.

Greta I'm glad to hear it. Then you will be all right. I always encourage loneliness.

Colette And that's how you see me, is it? In the future?

Greta I cannot see the future.

Colette I thought I could.

Greta But you were wrong.

Colette I was.

Greta Your dearest wish is to be a doctor?

Colette Yes.

Greta It is a noble one. I hope you succeed. Matthew will keep me informed. In the meantime, remember – you are alone, circling the earth, waiting to land. Who knows where and when? Perhaps never – perhaps nowhere.

Colette We can but live in hope. Don't tell me – you dislike hope.

Greta I could not have put it better myself. But I must thank you properly for being so attentive to my packing. Now, where is my purse? Is it in the suitcase?

Colette I didn't pack it.

Greta No, I have it here – I must. What is the point of searching for it? I do not have any Irish money in it. Only dollars and francs. And not that much of either, so I had better hang on to what I have. I will get Matthew to tip you for me. I can repay him when he next visits New York. He is so mean he is sure to remind me of what I owe him. And I am very Swedish in that way. I always pay my debts. I learned that as a youngster in Hollywood. Take nothing – absolutely nothing – that you have not earned – that is not your own anyway. Do you know what is the most base of all human feelings?

Colette What?

Greta Gratitude. Get away from here. Do what you have to do to be gone. Never come back, and succeed at any price.

Colette What did you get for doing that?

Greta America.

Colette What did it give you?

Greta It made me Garbo.

Colette Was it worth it?

Greta Nothing is ever worth it, but what is the alternative? Here is the alternative. Your aunt. A good heart. Never fall for it.

Paulie enters.

88

Paulie Is this a private conversation or can we all join in?

Greta My dear, I am corrupting your innocent niece with tales of old Hollywood. You have entered in the nick of time to stop me enticing her into a life of drudgery cleaning up after me. She has packed my luggage perfectly.

Paulie That's her job. It's what she's paid to do. I would hope, however, she does aspire to higher aims. Colette, stop pestering Miss Garbo with silly chat about films – you must have her head turned. Run down for your father. See if James is ready to set out in the car. Tell him they're packed and ready. Move – quick, quick.

Colette walks slowly out.

Keep her working – just keep her working – harsh, but the only remedy.

Greta For what?

Paulie Her heart's sore. She can't do medicine.

Greta Yes, she told me. Matthew and Harry did earlier, but I let her talk. She will manage. She has other dreams. They always do, the young. My flight to France is not until this evening. We should have plenty of time to reach the airport, yes?

Paulie Normally I'd say you would, but James was saying he might have to take a detour away from Derry. Some bother is stirring – there's a march over civil rights. Not the blacks – the Catholics. That's why James said you should start moving. So where is he? Typical man. Aren't they all the same? Never there when you need him.

Greta And you do, don't you? You and his wife. You need him. They are all the same, women.

Paulie Well, you're one as well.

Greta But men are not my – not my – I have no grasp of the word I'm seeking. Do you know? Perhaps you do and are hiding it from me. Are you? Tell me what you are hiding?

Paulie I offered to go to Dublin with her. With Colette. Pack up and do a runner. Settle somewhere in a flat or a small house. I'd get a job, keep the two of us, live cheap, and let her study. Qualify as a doctor just as she wished. She said no. She told me no. That wasn't the way she'd do it. So she turned down my offer. To help her. She mustn't have been as desperate as she claimed she was.

Greta But you were.

Paulie I just wanted to do what was best for her.

Greta How much would you give her? All you had?

Paulie shakes her head.

I'm glad to hear it – she might come back for more.

Paulie Would I offer it to her?

Greta You are a fool, and they say in English a fool and his money are soon parted.

Paulie Why am I a fool?

Greta You have not learned what is the wisest thing to do.

Paulie Which is?

Greta Say goodbye. I have always found that it is my happiest memory of people, bidding farewell.

Paulie You really are the great gloomy Swede.

Greta laughs.

Greta Didn't I tell you so?

Paulie They must love you at parties.

Greta They always ask me, I do accept – I never go.

Paulie Story of my life – I never did.

Greta Yes, that has saved you. Shyness – and slyness – like all little girls. You are a wise fool. So am I. Wise enough to know you will not kiss me goodbye. Never mind. That knowledge is enough of a kiss.

Sylvia enters.

Sylvia You'll never guess – wait until you hear. Sir Matthew walks up to James and do you know what he's after saying to him? He wants to bring Colette to Dublin with him and Harry and Miss Garbo. Isn't that brilliant? Let her see the place – give her a taste of the bright lights. So James is telling her now. I can't wait – I just cannot wait for all the excitement.

Colette enters.

Look at her – not able to speak with shock. Didn't I say the excitement would be mighty? It's not often my daughter is lost for words.

Paulie You better go and get ready, Colette.

Greta You are coming in the car?

Sylvia How else would she go?

Greta With us in the car? With me and Matthew and Harry?

Sylvia And with her father – James is driving.

Colette I don't want to go.

Greta That is not possible.

Sylvia It's a big car.

Colette I don't want to go in the first place.

Matthew and Harry enter, dressed for the journey.

Greta It is not possible. Matthew, you must do something. What were you thinking of? This cannot be allowed to happen. We cannot all of us travel to the airport in one car. It is not possible. Where shall I sit –?

Harry Surely we could squeeze – a tight fit, but –

Greta There is a solution. I hire another car.

Matthew I could not dream of allowing you –

Greta Harry, can you drive? Do I need to hire another driver? Is it possible to do this in the town? Is there a car rental?

Sylvia There is indeed – a second cousin of mine –

Greta I am indifferent to your cousins – how do I contact this firm? I dislike tight fits. I wish to drive in comfort.

Colette I said I don't want to go. Jesus, does anybody listen? The car is yours, yours entirely. You won't be contaminated by sitting next to me. I want to stay behind. Have fun in Dublin.

Colette exits, ignoring James as he enters.

James Is she all right?

Paulie She's grand. = Irish word for great

James There's something different about her today.

Paulie It's been a bit of an upheaval these past few days. She doesn't know if she is coming or going.

Sylvia I thought she would have loved to see Dublin.

Paulie You thought wrong.

Sylvia Maybe this is a good sign. Maybe she's getting it out of her system. She might stay at home.

Paulie Why should she? What is there for her here?

Sylvia Us.

James Her own.

Paulie She's had us all her life. She knows her own. She wants more. She's going to get some of what she wants. She's luckier than she thinks she is.

Sylvia Her aunt Paulie is helping us financially so Colette can train to be a teacher.

James Do you have to tell our business to strangers?

Sylvia Who are the strangers? Sir Matthew and Harry are our neighbours – and as for Greta Garbo, sure we'll never see you set foot in here again, will we?

Greta Fetch my luggage to the car. We should get a move on. I want to take one last look at the beautiful lake. Escort me, my handsome Harry. Be the gentleman. Fine memories, the perfect way to say goodbye.

Harry Do you dislike goodbyes?

Greta I love them. It's what I do best. Farewell.

Without her scarf, Greta exits with Harry.

Sylvia Did you ever hear the like? After all she's insulted me, she barks her orders into my face – fetch the luggage to her car. Well, before I move a muscle in her direction, she will be sitting with her hand held on her high hole for quite a while. Say what you like about me, but at least I have some pride about myself. Even in drink, I keep my dignity.

James Dignity – in drink? Woman, you'd lick it off a dead Christian brother.

Sylvia You're starting your disgusting chat early in the morning.

James It's the only way I can stick looking at your face.

Sylvia It has a long way to go before it's as ugly as yours.

James Enough of these pleasantries. I have my work to do. Will we make a start? We have a long drive ahead of us, Sir Matthew.

He lifts some luggage.

Sylvia I'll go to the door to see you off. Make sure you're out of sight.

James Make yourself useful. Take out the rest of the cases. If you look like a packhorse, act like one.

He exits, followed by Sylvia, complaining as she takes the remaining luggage.

Sylvia I might have known I'd be left with the heavier cases. It weighs a ton –

James Carry it – carry it – just carry it.

They are gone.
Matthew and Paulie share a brief silence.

Matthew They perform as expected, don't they – the loving couple?

Paulie And they are, Matt. A loving couple.

Matthew I know it. I'm sure they live only for each other.

Paulie Are you planning to come back?

Matthew I may.

Paulie Depends if you get a buyer in London or Dublin, does it?

Matthew I may be searching.

94

Paulie Greta's definitely not buying?

Matthew I didn't really think she would.

Paulie But you tried –

Matthew What else can one do? No, I should be pitching this establishment to a young couple – starting out – serenely Catholic – fertile as bejesus, ready to fill the rooms with delightful brats. A happy, noisy home, not full of your Hennessy bickering.

Paulie And this serenely happy and healthy couple – wherever you may find them –

Matthew I'm sure Ireland is crawling with these desirable creatures –

Paulie They won't be needing a housekeeper.

Matthew I doubt it, darling. Too expensive, on top of what I plan to charge them.

Paulie So I better keep my eyes open –

Matthew For a new post? That would be sensible, but not yet. Wait until we see. I would hate to lose you if I stayed. Harry's fond of you as well.

Paulie If you do come back, he'll be with you?

Matthew Ifs – ifs – so many ifs. Why do you ask? Are you so very fond of him?

Paulie All yours, Matthew. Everything is all yours – Harry, the house –

Matthew But Garbo – more yours, no?

She does not answer.

I should have used you more cleverly, my dear. Why did it not dawn on me you might be my secret weapon?

95

Paulie I'm afraid you've lost me.

Matthew You've made quite an impact.

Paulie I doubt that somehow.

Matthew She's bought you a painting.

Paulie What are you talking about?

Matthew Of the peacock. I've just finished it. She's paid in advance. Quite a few thousand. Have a peep of it in the studio. One of my best. Perhaps you would prefer the money. Put it into an educational trust. It would certainly last seven years. If you wish, I can sell it for you.

Paulie Matthew, if this is one of your cruel jokes –

Matthew That stubborn niece will go mad if she does not get her way. And it may be what we need. A doctor to tend us in our dotage. Not that she'll come back. As long as she lasts her first night in Dublin –

Paulie She's never been away from home – she'll weep buckets –

Matthew The Atlantic Ocean will cry from her eyes. But I know the rock she's cut from. She's tough enough to tackle those terrible matrons. Loads of practice. She'll survive – she has already.

Paulie How do you know that?

Matthew Haven't we?

Paulie You think so, Matt?

Matthew I do, Paulie – sometimes.

> *The horn of the car sounds.*
> *The horn of the car sounds again.*

Growing impatient to be gone. I must be off. Will you accept Greta's gift? What do I tell her?

Paulie That I wish her safe journey.

Matthew Good.

The horn of the car sounds a third time.

Greta must be panicking in case you rush out to –

Paulie In case I say more?

Matthew In case she sees you. She believes in control. Yes, you've made quite an impact. Mind the house.

Paulie Mind yourself.

He exits.
  She stands still in silence.
  She nearly breaks down but recovers.
  Sylvia enters.

They're gone?

Sylvia They're gone. Bag and baggage. Guess who showed up to wave them off?

Paulie Who?

Sylvia Our feathered friend that I would scalp. I thought it would make its beeline for me, but it just stood there, proud as punch, its tail spread out like a rainbow. The big smile on your one's face –

Paulie Greta?

Sylvia Who else? You'd think it came specially to see her. She did wave – big of her. I'm sure it was to the bloody peacock, not me. Where's Colette?

Paulie Stripping beds. There's news. Good news. Colette!

Sylvia Good news? Throw it in my direction – I've been starved of my fair share. What is it?

Paulie It concerns Colette.

Sylvia You can tell her mother.

Paulie I'd rather wait till she's here.

Colette enters.

Sylvia Your wait's over. She's present and correct. Your aunt Paulie is looking for you.

Colette What does she want?

Sylvia Ask her – she has a mouth can answer for herself.

Paulie sings.

Paulie
'I've just dropped in to see you all,
I'll only stay a while.
I want to see how you're getting on,
I want to see you smile.'

Sylvia What's got into that one?

Paulie continues singing.

Paulie
'And I'm happy to be back again
To greet you big and small,
For there's no place else on earth
Just like the homes of Donegal.'

Sylvia I'm glad somebody's happy.

Colette What do you want of me?

Paulie You're going to college –

Sylvia Tell us something we don't know.

Paulie To Dublin.

Colette I settled on that myself.

Paulie To study medicine.

Sylvia What are you talking about?

Paulie Medicine, Colette.

Sylvia We've had all this out – she'll be a teacher.

Paulie To study medicine, Colette.

Sylvia We haven't the money.

Paulie We have.

Sylvia How?

Paulie Greta. She's bought a painting from Sir Matthew. Bought it for us. He'll give us the cash instead –

Colette I don't want it.

Silence.

I don't want your painting.

Paulie How is it mine?

Colette She bought it from him for you. She knows it's what you most want in the world. She's giving it to you. Keep it.

Paulie Don't be a fool – don't turn up your nose –

Sylvia She doesn't want your leavings, Paulie, or anybody else's. She's saying, no.

Paulie Then she doesn't know what she's saying.

Colette You heard my mother. I'm saying, no. Thanks, but no.

Paulie You've taken leave of your senses. I thought all you ever wanted was –

Colette To stand on my own two feet. And I will – without Sir Matthew, and without Greta Garbo. Without you as well, Aunt Paulie. You don't have to provide for me. I don't want you to do that. I was going to have to say this one day. Better sooner than later.

Paulie Colette, this will break your heart.

Colette That's what happens to hearts.

Sylvia And she still has one to break.

Paulie For how much longer?

Colette That's for me to know, and the world to find out.

Colette exits.

Paulie There you go.

Sylvia There you go indeed.

Paulie You've won her.

Sylvia I doubt that. It's just that you've lost her. You'll get used to that. You'll survive the shock. You had it coming, Paulie. Manage – we all had to.

The peacock shrieks.

You still have your pal for company.

Paulie What am I going to do with a painting of a bloody peacock?

Sylvia Put a match to it, if that's what you want. Not that you will. It's a gift from your two admirers. Treasure it – you're proud as punch. Much good may it do you or them. They've thrown you a bone. Enjoy it. Don't pass it on to my daughter. She doesn't need it. She needs nobody. And do you know what, Paulie? Neither do you. Excuse me – I've work to do.

She sings.

'The time has come and I must go,
I bid you all adieu.'

She looks at Paulie.

Adieu then. Or as they say in these parts, so long. goodb

100

She exits.

Paulie So long, Sylvia. So long, the lot of you.

The peacock shrieks.

Give it a rest. We can hear you. Stop looking for attention. What's got into us altogether? Greta Garbo came to Donegal. Then she went away, leaving us as she found us. I want to be – what I want – whatever it was we were. Alone together. Goodbye, Greta. Goodbye, my boy. My beauty, adieu.

Colette enters with a bundle of laundry.

Colette Will we make a start on the washing?

Paulie What?

Colette The bedclothes – we should sort them.

Paulie We should.

The women sort the bedclothes for washing.
Greta enters as they go about their work.
She sees her scarf she has left behind.

Greta Here it is. Found. I knew I had not lost it. I need this for my journey.

Paulie The scarf? I would have posted it to you. I presume it must have been expensive.

Greta Cost three dollars – for two of them – in Macy's. Daylight robbery, but I took a shine to it. Why not spoil yourself?

Paulie Why not indeed? You have only one life.

Greta You look sad. I guess why. Colette has refused the gift.

She turns to Colette.

That is right, Colette?

Colette You actually remember my name?

Greta I remember everything. Especially those who said no to me. I always let them. Who was I to argue? What would be the point?

She turns to Paulie.

We should respect the young. They are without fear. She has made her decision. She will keep to it. Stand on her own two feet. Alone. That is good, isn't it? Paulie, am I right?

Paulie Aren't you always?

Greta Yes – it is a curse. But may I ask one question?

She turns to Colette.

Do you want to be a doctor?

Silence.

Is that what you want?

Colette Yes.

Greta Then go and be one. That is not advice. It is a warning. Others will destroy you. Do not destroy yourself. You understand me? Yes – you do, fully.

Colette breaks down.

Colette What will happen to them – my mother and my father?

Greta They will be with you to the end of the world. And beyond it. Why do you think you are weeping? Now, you will do as you are told?

Colette Yes.

Greta Ah, the Irish – so like the Swedes. Sheep.

Greta exits, without her scarf.

Colette I'm going then – to study medicine?

Paulie It seems like it.

Tentatively, Colette looks to embrace Paulie, who lets her.

Come on, my lady, we've work to do.

Colette We have.

Paulie Greta's delayed them. I hope they'll get through Derry quick. The big march will block the roads.

Colette They'll be grand. Daddy knows every inch of the city. He'll get them out of there in time.

Paulie Daddy, yes – the Rock of Gibraltar. We should steep these sheets.

Colette Look – she left her scarf behind again.

Paulie Did she?

Colette Will I run after the car?

Paulie Leave it. She said she had two, didn't she? Leave it.

Colette Right. Will I go up and run the water?

Paulie Do.

Colette exits, leaving Paulie still sorting sheets.
  She stops and wraps the scarf about herself.
  It suits her magnificently well.
  Music: Scott McKenzie, 'San Francisco'.
  The music is accompanied by the sound of water running, growing into a torrent, as Paulie, wearing the scarf, stands alone.